To dear Philip,
What else could I give you for your 25th. but a book like this one? Hope you enjoy it!
With fondest love
X Mir.

The Irresistible Impulse

To Barbara with love

The Irresistible Impulse

An Evocative Study of Erotic Notions and Practices Through the Ages

Norman Gelb

PADDINGTON
PRESS LTD
NEW YORK & LONDON

Library of Congress Cataloging in Publication Data
Gelb, Norman
   The irresistible impulse
   Includes index.
   1. Sex customs – History.   I. Title.
HQ12.G4   301.41′79   79–11624
ISBN 0 448 22368 6 (U.S. and Canada only)
ISBN 0 7092 0280 6

Filmset in England by Inforum Ltd., Portsmouth
Printed and bound in the United States

Designed by Patricia Pillay
Picture research by Georgina Barker

In the United States
PADDINGTON PRESS
Distributed by
GROSSET & DUNLAP

In the United Kingdom
PADDINGTON PRESS

In Canada
Distributed by
RANDOM HOUSE OF CANADA LTD.

In Southern Africa
Distributed by
ERNEST STANTON (PUBLISHERS) (PTY.) LTD.

In Australia and New Zealand
Distributed by
A.H. & A.W. REED

Contents

Acknowledgments

My thanks to the staffs of the British Museum Library, the London Library and the London public library system – particularly the Fulham branch – for their assistance and courtesy; to Glorya Hale for her advice and encouragement; to Norman Moss for his perceptive criticism of the manuscript (though all shortcomings of the book are my own responsibility); to Georgina Barker for her help in accumulating the illustrations; to my editor, Emma Dally, for her encouragement and assistance; to Mallary and Amos who put up with me while this book took shape; most of all to my wife whose idea this book was and whose advice, criticism and support were invaluable from beginning to end.

Preface

WE LIVE, we are told, in a sex-obsessed age. Our sexual appetites are said to be perpetually aroused by an all-pervasive erotic atmosphere. Sexual performance is said to be a major concern of just about everybody these days.

We also live in an age of exaggeration, of which the above assessment is a prime example. Nevertheless, sex has become distinctly respectable and fashionable of late. It has become a symbol of personal fulfillment, something about which to boast or to feel private exaltation. It is undeniably a major theme of our times.

However, as the following pages illustrate, sex – though a normal, natural function – has consistently been a central focus of the human imagination. There have even been eras as sex-obsessed as our own, in different ways perhaps, but in ways which were often more spectacular.

This book traces the development of sexuality in our civilization. It explores shifting patterns and quirks, fads and fancies, of erotic behavior over the ages. It shows how people at different times reconciled prevailing fashions and moral codes with their irrepressible sexual impulses – much as we are doing today. Like sex itself, this sexual evolution has been an extraordinary adventure. Like sex itself, it has been exciting, bewildering at times, and totally entrancing.

The Irresistible Impulse

Sexual pleasure, widely used and not abused, may prove the stimulus and liberation of our finest and most exalted activities.

— HAVELOCK ELLIS

I'll wager you that in ten years it will be fashionable again to be a virgin.

— BARBARA CARTLAND

Sex is something I really don't understand too hot. You never know where the hell you are.

— J.D. SALINGER, *Catcher in the Rye*

SEX HAS ALWAYS been a giddy game – one which nature plays with us and one which we play with each other. For many men and women, no pleasure can match it, no indulgence is more thrilling. Some consider sex the only really worthwhile human pursuit and pursue it with unwavering determination. Even those who are not obsessed with sex consider it one of life's great adventures – a magical private joy, an ongoing challenge, or reassuring therapy in an otherwise insufficiently responsive world.

Even during periods of rigid puritanical restraint, when sex was denounced as wicked and depraved, the human sexual urge invariably proved indomitable. The sexual imagination has always ranged from inexhaustible to feverish, often adapting dramatically to challenging circumstances.

Past repressive periods, for example, had rich threads of sensuality woven intricately into the fabric of the times. In days which were subsequently "cleansed" and glorified, knights like those seated by legend around King Arthur's famous Round Table were, in fact, more easily moved to lechery than chivalry. They regularly bedded down not only their supposedly untouchable ladies fair but, given half a chance, all other desirable damsels they happened to encounter as well.

In a later period, when relentless moralists and witchfinders were haranguing women for distracting men with their carnal attractions, thus leading virtue down the road to damnation, celebrated artists were immortalizing naked images of voluptuous females, and were acclaimed for it.

Less than a century ago, when the facts of respectable Victorian life were that sex was unmentionable and degenerate, and when properly-raised young women grew up with a nameless dread of their wedding nights, whorehouses did a booming business in every major city in the world.

Sex has had a turbulent history all of its own. Developments in recent years testify as much. A few years ago, young women appealed to "advice to the lovelorn" columnists in newspapers for guidance on when to surrender their first kiss. Now they consult experts on radio "phone in" programs on what sort of contraceptive to use. As recently as 1959, D.H. Lawrence's novel, *Lady Chatterley's Lover*, with its portrayal of sexual desire and fulfillment, just managed to squeak past courtroom charges of obscenity. Today, it (and books even more explicit) is required reading in college English classes. Not long ago, doctors who probed the mysteries of sexuality were popularly dismissed as dirty-minded quacks. Now, eminently respectable *sexologists* and institutes of sexology come equipped with impressive academic credentials.

Clearly, there has been a sweeping transformation in attitudes toward sex. Not only is it now unanimously and unabashedly conceded that sexual indulgence is not necessarily immoral, but chastity, once extolled ("dear to heaven," the poet John Milton called it), is increasingly dismissed as a sexual deviation, perhaps even a perversion.

This mood is, of course, mirrored in the permissive current attitudes toward erotica – in print, in art, in movies and on television. But, aside from usually brief repressive periods, sexual themes have, in fact, repeatedly been expressed in art clear across the vast expanse of human history. Remains of the earliest examples of human art reveal that cave men carved sexual images, concentrating primarily on female erogenous regions. Erotic imagery, including the portrayal of copulation, had religious significance in ancient Egypt and other early civilizations. Sexually provocative paintings and carvings peered daringly out from the deep shadows of the Dark Ages, were exhibited boldly in subsequent periods, and have continued to be a major focus of artistic inspiration.

To trace erotica back to its origins is to explore a prodigious range of human experience. Far from being the depraved product of overindulgent societies – as is sometimes claimed – erotica is more venerable than civilization itself. No besotted Sodom, no permissive age, no warping of respectable standards was required to set the stage for sexually provocative art. Like sex itself, it sprang full-grown from the human condition. What is unique about our own age is that never before has erotica been so easily accessible to vast numbers of people.

And never before has so much energy been expended in analyzing, describing and debating the sexual antics of humans – who does what with whom, why, in what way, and how often. In addition to creative erotica and journalistic forays into sexuality, an immense amount of genuine scholarship is now devoted to all varieties of sexual behavior. The physiology of the sex act is meticulously examined. Statistics on copulation, masturbation, homosexuality and bestiality are compiled, analyzed and regularly updated. Intriguing comparisons are drawn between the habits and capabilities of humans and other animals. One such analysis – a scrupulously scientific study – notes dryly, for example, that, "In the fully erect condition, the organ (of the human male) has an average length of 6¼ inches. . . . There are no measurements for the engorged gorilla phallus. . . ."

Like just about everything else even remotely associated with sexuality, the significance of erotic humor as a mirror of the times has been explored, notably in *The Rationale of the Dirty Joke* by Gershon Legman. He relates one story of a witness at a rape trial who is rebuked by the judge for offending the court by using the vernacular word for copulation, and who replies:

> *His pants were down, his arse was bare,*
> *His balls were hanging in midair,*
> *His you-know-what was you-know-where,*
> *If that wasn't fucking, I wasn't there.*

But the elevation of sex through familiarity to its proper place as a normal aspect of human activity and interest has, perversely, failed to eliminate the complications which can be part of the sexual adventure. Despite its undeniable pleasures, sex remains a conundrum. It can be an exalting experience, but it can also befuddle emotions, confuse relationships and even at times disrupt mental balance. It has been acclaimed as the supreme joy and condemned as the supreme evil. It has been in and out of respectable fashion over the ages – and we are *still* not absolutely sure what sex is all about.

It is baffling that something as normal as sex can be so complex, that something so naturally ordained can continue to be so controversial, that something so much a part of our lives can be probed and dissected by so many psychiatric treatises and "how-to" manuals.

The blame is attributable to the dichotomy between the pleasure of sex and its other dimension – the one which has taken precedence in the greater scheme of things: sex has always been essential for the perpetuation of the human race. It is the means by which we have produced offspring to

11

maintain our presence on Earth, our ongoing significance, our link with posterity.

Though fashioned by nature as a lure, a come-on, a regard for going through the procreative act, carnal delights have also posed fundamental potential dangers. Threats of disruption of community harmony through jealousy, dereliction of work duty in hard-pressed societies, breakdown of population control, and possible disapproval of capricious deities led to the early emergence of restrictive codes of sexual behavior. But such codes clash with sexual impulses and have, as a consequence, never been fully accepted. Confusions over what is tolerable and what is not in erotic behavior have persisted right through history. They exist right now. What forms of sexual pleasure, if any, are obscene, morally corrupt or just in bad taste? What rights has the community to decide which forms of sexual behavior and public erotic display should not be tolerated? Is the "perfect orgasm" attainable by just about everybody (as some sexologists contend) and, if it is, what moral codes and loyalties can individuals rightly violate to attain it?

These questions are framed in the modern world, but examples can be cited of the problems of comprehension and acceptance which sexuality has posed in the past and of how our forbears tried to cope with them. Primitive peoples, for example, associated sexual excitement with magical forces and spirits which governed their universe, for whom they copulated ceremonially in tribute. The ancient Greeks at first constructed an edifice of erotic imagery around their gods and goddesses, who could cope more readily than humans with ecstasies which confounded both feelings and reason. The Romans, sober and practical, imperial engineers still unmatched, were direct in their approach to everything and made no great fuss about sex, except for uncharacteristic, periodic, explosive orgiastic festivals.

During the Middle Ages, sex-crazed abstinents scourged themselves mercilessly to eradicate abominable carnal urges which contaminated their immortal souls. Faced with the requirements of human survival and the tenacity of the sexual impulse, medieval theologians were forced to turn doctrinal somersaults and, in due course, concluded that sex was not in truth objectionable, provided no pleasure was derived from it. There were obvious problems with that formula and moralists were later able to grant that sex could indeed be enjoyable, so long as it was not promiscuous. With the passage of time, libertarians appeared on the scene to assert that nothing was really wrong with promiscuity if it liberated the human spirit.

As women as well as the human spirit became liberated, new frontiers of sexuality were crossed. Many women became less willing to accept subservient roles to men in sexual relations, or anything else. Both the extent and the lasting effects of the women's liberation campaign are still to be gauged. But the development of easily practiced, effective contraception (recent reports tell of work on developing an effective contraceptive nasal spray) has now increased the opportunity for women to enjoy a kind of sexual freedom they have never since the beginning of human life on Earth experienced. As the implications sink in, both men and women will have to adjust to a totally new sexual environment.

The sexual revolution, about which so much has been written lately, has, in fact, not yet occurred. It is just around the corner. This account begins, however, with the earlier sexual revolution, the one in which our primordial ancestors participated millions of years ago, to set the stage for everything else that has happened in the fiery annals of the human sexual experience.

The Dawn People

The Dawn People

*If you watch lizards and lions copulating, then you will see that in
200,000,000 years the male has not had a single new idea. He still
approaches (the female) from the rear, probably grasps her neck in his
teeth and has done with it in short order.*

— ROBERT ARDREY, *The Hunting Hypothesis*

UNLIKE OTHER ANIMALS, humans have always had new ideas
about sex. As far back as records go, there is evidence that
men and women are capable of a wide range of erotic notions
and practices. In their fantasies, in their varieties of carnal
play and coupling, in their social posturing, they have shown
over the ages that their sexual imagination is spirited and
vigorous, often exotic and sometimes bizarre.

Erotic art, which has been a feature of human endeavor
since prehistoric times, and erotic literature have repeatedly
demonstrated that, of all living creatures, only men and
women can turn their brains into self-stimulating erogenous
zones. Saintly hermits, removed geographically from temptations of the flesh, have flayed themselves bloody in vain
efforts to banish lascivious thoughts. Scrutineers of our
psychological make-up have defined all kinds of seemingly
non-erotic human behavior and thought in terms of sexual
urges. Street corner newsstands the world over flaunt sexually
titillating girlie magazines which sell spectacularly well in our
permissive age – when such vicarious thrills might reasonably
be considered superfluous. The enormous interest in
periodic sweeping surveys of "normal" and "deviant" sexual
behavior suggests that more than merely academic interest is
involved.

16

The fact is humans are uniquely erotic animals, profoundly and often incessantly committed to sexuality. During their evolutionary emergence millions of years ago, humans even proved to be sexual wizards, literally turning sex around.

Their evolutionary forebears in the animal kingdom engaged in rear-entry copulation, the male of the species penetrating the female from behind, as virtually all animals still do. Men and women, however, found this front-to-back coupling unsatisfactory and inadequate for human purposes. They chose instead to face each other for their sexual encounters. It was a major development in the history of living things. It laid the groundwork for both our erotic obsessions and, arguably, for civilization as well.

Despite the subservience of woman to man over the ages, this sexual revolution was her doing. Dawn woman faced a unique challenge in fulfilling her distinctive biological role. To perpetuate the human race, she had to improve the chances of survival of the helpless babies she bore, offspring who required her close attention for more than a year and who needed further care for more than a decade – while she was having more babies.

The quills of baby porcupines harden so that they can go foraging for their own food after a few hours of life. Gnu calves can keep up with the moving herd when they are a few days old. Harp seal pups are left on their own on ice floes to sink or swim after about three weeks. A baby gorilla can fend for itself after eight months. But human females, with their vulnerable progeny, carry a much more demanding instinctive maternal burden than the females of other species. Dawn woman required a fundamental metamorphosis of which almost all other animals were incapable or did not find necessary in their own evolutionary development.

Despite their often extravagant courtship rituals (hippotamuses ram each other at full speed; hares practically rape their mates), animals other than humans copulate only to reproduce. Their sexual behavior is biologically attuned to that function, as is demonstrated by the calendar timing of their sexual activity. The females of other animal species are

17

sexually astir for restricted periods – some, like apes, a week each month; some, like dogs, twice a year; some, like wild sheep, once a year. When these animals are not in heat, they are neither attractive nor receptive to males.

Males and females of some animal species live in mutually exclusive sexual ghettos most of the year. After being impregnated, the females of these species congregate in groups from which the males are driven off and kept away. Courtship and copulation occur between the sexes in the animal kingdom only when conception is a biological possibility. There are no exceptions or lapses. It would be physically impossible. When it does occur, copulation between animals is rarely part of a lasting relationship.

Such a pattern of transitory sexual involvement is possible by choice for humans in today's social climate. But it would have been impossible for dawn woman as she evolved from a pre-human ape-like form, capable of caring for herself, into a vulnerable creature, squandering much of her energy on raising her infants. Sexual communism, without pairing off and with free mating within the protective group (such as is common among some ape species in which infants mature quickly), may have been practiced and found wanting in the course of human social evolution. But to guarantee the survival of budding humanity, dawn woman created her own sexual conditions. Ironically, those conditions were destined to be the basis of her subservient role in the man-woman relationship from that point forward. She did it for the children.

The earliest man-woman bond was fashioned by the woman's need for a reliable and constant provider over a long period of time. It had to be someone who was not liable to be incapacitated by pregnancy or child rearing, someone who would return to her and her children from the hunt or from foraging. There had to be an enduring link upon which she could depend. That link was forged through expanding the purpose of sexual attraction. For *homo sapiens* – still in the process of adapting to human physical and mental capabilities – copulation ceased to be a purely biological exercise with some temporarily diverting courtship flourishes. It was imbued with social meaning and came to serve a socially useful purpose. It became the basis of the family unit, as well as the means for perpetuating mankind.

Fundamental biological alterations made the change possible. Having evolved from creatures which were only occasionally in heat, the human female became sexually available and sexually attractive to a consort-provider all the year round. She could establish a claim to his enduring affection, loyalty and protection by always being able to satisfy his sexual needs and proprietorial instincts. She became something to come home to, even when that home was only a cave or a makeshift encampment on a savannah.

Development of human bodies for frontal rather than rear-entry copulation intensified the man-woman bond. It gave to each a greater identity and clearer personality in the eyes of the other. It further secured the potentially footloose and promiscuous "husband" to the vulnerable "wife" (and, incidentally, helped eliminate the element of violent competition common among many species of male animals at mating time).

Thus was born the emotion known as love (better called *romantic* love to distinguish it from other forms of profound affection between individuals). Stable family life and biological alterations tended to regularize human sexual behavior. The oral area grew more intensely erogenous, the kiss probably developing from the instinctive love bite of animals. For sexual signaling, woman's breasts developed beyond the suckling needs of her babies. Though most ape-like body hair was shed, pubic hair was retained to reduce friction during copulation. Unlike the females of other species, woman remained receptive to men even during most of her pregnancy.

It was unlikely, however, that primal man and woman were obsessed with sex, despite year-round female receptivity and the attractions of other cosmetic biological developments. The environment in which humans evolved was nothing like the Garden of Eden. Survival was the primary task. Most energy was devoted to finding food – either wild edible plants

19

or game (among the formidable creatures which Stone Age man hunted were mammoth elephants and giant boars). During glacial periods, and there were several during the emergence of *homo sapiens*, temperatures even in areas remote from ice-bound regions plummeted. Survival for fledgling humans became even more of a challenge.

Cold and subsistence living have always had a dulling effect on erotic impulses. The concentration on day-to-day existence probably confined Stone Age sexual performance to the simple, hasty gratification of unembellished animal urges. (When chimpanzees copulate, the time which elapses between mounting and ejaculation is rarely more than ten seconds. For lions, it is usually between five and ten seconds.)

Nevertheless, this harsh environment spawned mankind's first works of erotic art. Sexual themes in art have been persistent and widespread virtually from the beginning of man's conscious effort to record his presence on Earth. The earliest of these artists – men who carved erotic stone figurines and decorated cave walls with erotic images – were Neolithic creatures, cave dwellers and big game hunters of the Stone Age, just a few branches up the evolutionary tree from their (and our) pre-human forebears. They lived between 20,000 and 35,000 years ago, before humanity had begun toying with metal and before it had deciphered the mysteries of agriculture. They left traces of their existence and achievements in a scattering of isolated sites across southern and central Europe, western Asia, North Africa and various other locations which have since become shrines for archaeologists, anthropologists and aesthetes.

Art was never more significant as a means of communicating ideas and feelings than before the invention of writing. It was then the only way to convey thoughts and moods to those who were not present, to posterity or to whatever deities and spirits were feared and revered. Surviving relics of those prehistoric times offer an intriguing insight into the sexual imagination of Stone Age man.

Though images of his masculine contemporaries, with

phalluses erect, have been unearthed, reproductions of the female form predominate, with the focus on prodigious bosoms, generous thighs and prominently displayed genitalia. These were the erogenous features of the female anatomy which had first induced the primitive hunter to provide and care for his mate and which have remained the primary foci of interest of eroticists ever since. These were unmistakable, undisguised sex objects signaling mankind's conscious erotic awakening.

If artistic delicacy was sometimes missing from these works, explicitness was not. Cave men carved the earliest-known sexual graffiti and the first pinups in history on the rock walls of their shelters. There were repeated representations of the vulva – small, vertical gashes in the rock, enveloped by slightly raised surfaces. These occur too often in Paleolithic sites to be either accidental or misinterpreted. But fully realized figurines and carvings of nude females are even more revealing. Large bosoms and ample thighs are hallmarks of the Stone Age artist's idealized vision of the female form. A carving of a buxom woman holding a bison horn found at Laussel in France and a figurine of an even more amply endowed female found at Willendorf in Austria are notable evidence that lush sexual zones provided the artist with his primary definition of femininity. On the wall of a cave at Camargue in France, the pubic triangle serves as the center of focus of a leisurely reclining female who would not be out of place in a modern erotic painting.

Like many of their subsequent colleagues, those who first used sexual imagery in art conjured up fantasies when fashioning their creations. The shape of their extravagantly proportioned *Venuses* (so called by the archaeologists who discovered them) were no closer to the shape of real women than are the voluptuous caricatures in present-day bawdy cartoons. In any case, it probably would have been too cold in many of the places where they have been found for the females whose likenesses they carved or painted to pose unclad.

Intriguingly, the Paleolithic artists who created the Venuses seem to have paid little attention to the faces of their female figures. Though time and erosion may have obliterated some of those faces, most seem to have been left originally blank or indistinguishable. Facial beauty appears to have been a quality still to be discovered or, at the time, played no role in artistic erotic portrayal. So, too, later periods and places were to develop erotic fashions of their own which, for example, emphasized the daintiness of women's feet in old China or boyish bosoms in the "flapper" 1920s.

It is highly likely that the Stone Age figurines, many just a few inches high, were carved in daylight, the artists laboriously chipping away at chunks of rock with primitive stone implements until their provocative Venuses took shape. But darkness within the caves probably meant that drawings and carvings on cave walls had to be cooperative efforts, with the artists needing light and assisted by fire tenders and fuel bearers. In view of climatic and other external restraints on sexual activity, their calculated exertions and achievements, transforming erotic fantasy into visual imagery, were significant milestones in the development of the human imagination.

In some cases, there may have been mystical inducements for erotic imagery. There is much speculation among scholars about a *Mother Goddess* or *Earth Goddess*, a goddess of fertility whom Stone Age (and later) humans may have worshiped and whom they sought to depict in their erotic carvings, paintings and scratchings. Certainly in the next stage of human development, specific forms of erotic display were widely considered crucial to survival.

Between 11,000 and 9,000 years ago, general climatic improvement, the extinction of some species of big game upon which hunting groups survived, and the development of new skills, led to the emergence of arable farming and livestock breeding. This prelude to civilization was accompanied by a new catalogue of survival-linked erotic activities. The continued existence of men and women depended on animals and crops. A bad harvest was a disaster. So was a shortfall of domesticated cattle or game. An abundance of all three was ideal. In a world governed by mysterious, often capricious forces, encouragement of crop and animal fertility by whatever means available was deemed not only proper, but absolutely essential as well.

Sympathetic magic – the procedure for invoking an act by imitating it – is not unknown today. But it was common among primitive peoples. Simulating the sexual antics of lusty bulls and rams and their receptive cows and ewes was, for Neolithic stockbreeders, an intoxicating encouragement to the all-powerful forces of nature. It diminished, most pleasurably, the danger that their herds might refrain from sexual indulgence and become barren. In crop-farming communities, men and women imitated the impregnation of the Earth with seed, assuring, most agreeably, that crops would flourish.

In time, these practices became religious rituals and, as fertility rites, grew into elaborate communal charades involving sexually stimulating dancing, other orgiastic displays and public copulation. They became erotic festivals, designed to please and appease the spirits and forces which governed human existence. "We may assume," anthropologist Sir James Frazer wrote, "that the profligacy which notoriously attended these ceremonies was an essential part of worship."

Though these festivities were among the earliest forms of organized worship, many of the rituals, in altered form, have survived the passage of time. Early in the twentieth century, peasant men and women in eastern Europe still lay down and rolled chastely over the fields at sowing time to guarantee good harvests, while priests, never suspecting the erotic origin of the practice, blessed them and their crops.

Primitive fertility rites varied from region to region. In Bengal, orgies to arouse the Earth Mother were preceded by the chanting of suggestive songs. In Central America, seeding the fields and ritual copulation took place simultaneously as interlocking rather than consecutive rites. In Peru, fertility festivals were highlighted by orgiastic displays. In Burma, ritualistic defloration of virgins was believed to assure crop fertility.

The western tradition of the spring bride dates back to a time when she was less a bride in the conventional sense and more a proxy for the Earth spirit, aroused and penetrated by a human planter as an example and a prod to nature. Kissing the bride at weddings probably originated in much more intimate ceremonial relations between the chosen female fertility image and the men of her community. (In some primitive mideastern cultures, it was the practice for the bride to lay with the male wedding guests before the husband exercised his conjugal rights.) Queen of May celebrations on May Day, later to become charming, quaint and antiseptic, may have had similar origins as this English doggerel suggests:

> *The first of May,*
> *The first of May,*
> *Outdoor fucking begins today.*

Male participants in primitive fertility festivals sometimes wore animal masks to accentuate the symbolic nature of the rites. Rock carvings dating back 7,000 years have been found in Fezzan in Libya depicting masked males with enormous, erect phalluses. One man, dog-masked, is shown copulating with a woman who has spread her legs wide to ease his penetration.

Genitals become symbols of procreation. Images of the penis and testicles, and of the vulva, became objects of veneration, talismans and decorative household objects. Chalk phalluses dating back 4,000 years have been found in southern England, not far from the naked giant of Cerne Abbas, a huge relic of Roman Britain, etched into the countryside. (Even in recent times, women hoping to become pregnant slept the night on its erect phallus.) Rock sketches in the Camonica Valley in northern Italy and elsewhere show warriors with erections while in battle, additional testimony to their manliness.

The males of other animal species also sometimes aggressively flaunt their masculinity. But this behavior was first recorded in humans in societies which were already growing increasingly intricate and laced with complex codes and procedures. It was in this realm that sex would play a role far more significant than might have been expected from so routine a biological imperative. Sexual behavior and display were being molded by the impact of emergent civilization, and they would color that emergence with distinctive hues all their own.

Not till later would the sexual environment be bathed in intrigue, with the image of erotic display fluctuating between what was sophisticated and what was unseemly, between the chic and the obscene. Not till later would, for example, the more canny of beautiful courtesans of ancient Greece up-end their hourglasses to time the visits of their clients. Not till later still would community dignitaries indulge in private sexual pastimes of the kind they felt obliged publicly to condemn.

A hint of the confusions and distractions in store was apparent soon enough, when sexual display emerged from the mysteries of Stone Age obscurity into the magic of ritual and belief of early civilizations. But while that transformation was in progress, erotic display was deemed a necessary community service whose importance would never subsequently be duplicated: it consciously helped sustain human existence.

Erotic Worship

Erotic Worship

. . . at Babylon, every woman, whether rich or poor, had once in her life to submit to the embraces of a stranger at the temple of Mylitta . . . and to dedicate to the goddess the wages earned by this sanctified harlotry. The sacred precint was crowded with women waiting to observe the custom. . . . At Heliopolis . . . the custom of the country required that every maiden should prostitute herself to a stranger at the temple of Astarte, and matrons as well as maids testified their devotion to the goddess in the same manner.

– SIR JAMES FRAZER, *The Golden Bough*

IN THE ANCIENT world the name of the goddess to whom sexual tribute was paid varied from place to place. But the erotic content of religious worship was explicitly evident in such sanctified copulation with strangers. The practice was widespread and was only one of several elements of religious sexuality common at the time. As civilization took root, sexual rituals were, as in primitive times, fundamental to religious devotion. Those rituals included the worship of the penises of various gods and the consecrated ceremonial coupling of kings and priestesses.

A number of religious celebrations, like that at the temple of Hathor, ancient Egypt's goddess of love and joy and guardian of women, ended in sexual free-for-alls. At harvest festivals in Phoenicia, women could choose between shaving their heads in annual mourning for the god of vegetation or offering themselves sexually to strangers – neither option was considered degrading.

At a time when religious observance played a central role in day-to-day life, the commitment to sexuality in worship was guiltless and casual. The earliest written symbols for male and female in Sumeria – important innovations – were simply lines representing the penis and the vulva.

Gods and goddesses of fertility, for whose greater glory primitive humans had frolicked in rustic orgies (and still would for a long time to come in cultural backwaters), did not readily relinquish their hold on the popular imagination. Societies grew more complex and people grew more sophisticated, but the erotic demands of those deities – as interpreted by priests and priestesses – continued to stimulate erotic cravings, appetites and superstitions.

The earliest great civilizations were, however, to provide a setting for a major transformation. The emphasis in erotic display was to shift from religion to sensual pleasure, from worship to personal rapture. Public sexuality was to become secularized and, under certain circumstances, was to pose a threat to prevailing standards of morality.

As the first agrarian communities grew stable and expanded, codes of personal behavior were refashioned to meet new conditions. They were designed to bolster group stability by eliminating or curtailing disruptive pressures. Murder and theft were outlawed. Rules were formulated to facilitate amicable settlement of disputes within the community. Promiscuity, a danger to stable community life, was curbed.

Group marriage, in which several men and women had sexual access to each other without individual members of the group living together as husband and wife, faded away. Taboos against incest, which compelled individuals to marry outside their own families, eliminating a potential cause of domestic disruption and promoting the formation of wider protective and productive alliances, were cloaked in cautionary folklore. So were prohibitions against adultery. Even in recent times, it was widely believed among some primitive hunting tribes that a wife's infidelity jeopardized the success of a husband's hunting expedition and even exposed him to the danger of being killed by wild animals. With sexual indulgence believed to be linked to supernatural spirits, sexual taboos retained religious overtones.

Clothing also played an interesting role in early erotic development. Anthropologist Edward Westermarck said they owed their origin (where weather was not a factor) to "the desire of men and women to make themselves attractive." With the onset of the civilizing process, they began to serve the purpose of modesty rather than that of sexual stimulation.

Confident of survival within the group, people could focus increasingly on aspects of life other than survival. Although a key development in the emergence of civilization, this inevitably produced various complexities. Religious worship continued to be a central focus of existence. But it took on increasingly intricate trappings, with elaborate temples and hosts of priests. Previously rustic magical-mystical worship of deities became a complex body of ritual and belief. Formerly uncomplicated sexual tribute to fertility deities took on detailed meaning and symbolism, providing worshipers with new forms of religious erotic stimulation.

Erotic references, particularly to the penis, abounded in the earliest organized religions, notably in ancient Egypt. The sun was considered god of the penis. The Earth itself was believed to have developed from a drop of hardened semen. Geb, lord of the Earth, and Nut, goddess of the sky, copulated endlessly until pried apart, after which they longed endlessly to be reunited in carnal embrace. Min, a fertility god, was commonly represented in statues and murals with penis erect. The penis of Osiris, Egypt's god of the lower world and benefactor of mankind, was an important religious symbol. The annual Nile floods, which kept Egypt's fields fertile, were believed to be Osiris's life-creating semen. At festival time, women in Nile villages paraded effigies of the god, manipulating its enormous phallus with strings.

The world saw the initial blossoming of literary erotica in Egypt and Mesopotamia. It was there about 5,000 years ago that sexuality was given its first written, enduring words. They were etched on tablets and stones which were to be discovered and deciphered thousands of years later. On one such tablet, a

Mesopotamian fertility goddess is quoted as asking plain-
tively, "Who will be my plowman? My vulva is ready." Another
fragment records the first known rape, inflicted on an Earth
goddess by a rain god who ignored her protests that "my vulva
is small."

Less coy was Ishtar, the Babylonian fertility goddess. In
addition to inspiring carnal desire between others, Ishtar took
mortal lovers whom she exhausted physically. No doubt such
erotic legends had been transmitted orally from generation to
generation before the written word was invented to transcribe
them. Like legends elsewhere, they no doubt reflected human
experiences, desires and fantasies.

In the Babylonian *Gilgamesh* epic, dating back some 4,000
years, erotic impulses were seen to have a civilizing influence,
with the man-savage Enkidu tamed by a girl:

> She untied her loin cloth and opened her legs and he
> took her. She did not resist but accepted his ardor. . . .
> She used on him a woman's wiles. And his love was drawn
> into her.

After that mesmerizing experience, Enkidu forsook the
companionship of the wild animals with whom he had grown
up and turned instead to human ways. (Later, in more
hidebound periods, kindness or harsh discipline rather than
sexual inducements would be recommended for taming wild
spirits.)

A few surviving fragments indicate that there was a blossoming of delicate, sensual literary imagery in ancient Egypt.
There are references to the vulva as a gentle trap for the penis
and to the splendor of women's breasts. Tender erotic moods
were invoked:

> *I am with you and lift up my heart.*
> *Do we not embrace and fondle each other*
> *when you visit me*
> *And we surrender to delights?*

In earlier days, kings in the ancient world had often
assumed divine status among their subjects. It went with the

31

job. They also assumed some of the obligations and duties of deities, including those of fertility gods. Rulers in Mesopotamia engaged in sacred copulation with priestesses each autumn to restore the fertility of nature after the blazing summer sun had seared the fields. Similarly, early pharaohs of Egypt publicly straddled their queens at crop-sowing time, planting their own seed as an encouragement to nature. Fertility rites pure and simple, these were also an extension of sex into the realm of politics, linking the fertility of the land with the king's person and potency – an early equivalent of an election promise.

Religious prostitution was the most prevalent remnant of primitive fertility rituals. In honor of fertility deities, women made themselves sexually available to men in places of worship and received token payment for their gestures. Herodotus wrote that every Babylonian woman had to sit in the temple of the goddess of fertility "and there give herself to a strange man. . . . Once a woman has taken her seat, she has to wait there until a man has thrown a silver coin into her lap and taken her outside to lie with her. . . . The woman has no privilege of choice – she must accompany the first man who casts money her way."

The influence of fertility deities spread far and wide. The Greek geographer Strabo noted that still during his lifetime (63 BC-AD19) the most illustrious citizens of Cappadocia, in what is now Turkey, offered their daughters to the service of a fertility goddess before they were married – just as illustrious citizens of later cultures would encourage their daughters to dabble in social work. Sir James Frazer recorded that "in Armenia, the noblest families dedicated their daughters to the service of the goddess Anaitis in her temple . . . where the damsels acted as prostitutes for a long time before they were given in marriage." Eli, high priest of the Israelites, is said in the Old Testament (1 Samuel 2:22) to have been distressed to hear "that his sons . . . lay with women that assembled at the door of the tabernacle of the congregation" at a time when the monotheistic Israelites, whose God abhorred such practices, were subjected to particularly strong external influences.

Sanctified prostitution had developed gradually with the emergence of civilization. As early farming communities became villages and as those villages became the embryos of great cities and city-states, primitive erotic festivals had to be updated. Ceremonial public debauchery in the fields, designed to keep the crops growing, the ritual flaunting of penises and vulvas, though still prevalent long afterward in agrarian regions, was hardly suitable in the sophisticated cities of Babylon and Thebes, with their ornate palaces, thriving commercial enterprises and learned philosophers toying with mathematics and astronomy. Erotic tribute to the appropriate gods and goddesses was still essential. But it had to be urbanized and slotted into its proper niche. This was partly done by recourse to consecrated whoredom within the precints of the temples.

Secular prostitution – practiced by women who made no pretense of spiritual motives – may have been an outgrowth of religious prostitution, though the two probably developed side by side. The Zoroastrians of ancient Persia called the legendary first woman "the Demon Whore" and considered her a threat to man's dignity. But in Mesopotamia, secular whores, like religious prostitutes, were considered devotees of fertility deities, worshiping in the same way, though living off the proceeds.

Whichever came first, prostitution appears to have been practiced ever since man emerged as a creature of commerce, buying and selling things. There were men in Babylon who grew rich peddling the favors of their slave girls. (Pimping has been called the world's second oldest profession.) Men and women who ran taverns in the cities of Mesopotamia had a reputation for using them as brothels as well, and men seeking the services of prostitutes knew where to go to find them. Joshua's spies, scouting out the city of Jericho for the Israelites, were not surprised to stumble across the whore, Rahab, who hid them when they were being hunted. Samson seemed to have encountered no difficulty in locating the harlot he "went in onto" (Judges 16:1). In Assyria and some other places, prostitutes were not required to go veiled in public

33

places as were respectable women, and sometimes were forbidden to.

Outside the realm of prostitution, lascivious behavior was sufficiently common to influence the content of the earliest known written laws in Mesopotamia. Greatly concerned with the protection of private property, those laws reveal how deeply adultery was felt to be a menace to man's dominance over his wife, who was considered his property. It was theft. An adulterous wife could be divorced for her transgression, and could also be put to death, though no punishment was specified for the adulterous husband – unless his adultery was with a married woman. (According to the code of Hammurabi, king of Babylon, among other legitimate grounds for divorcing a wife were her failure to bear children and the squandering of her husband's wealth.) The biblical Ten Commandments ruled that adultery was a sin without specifying the sex of the transgressing adulterer, though nowhere in the Old Testament is a man who copulated with concubines considered sinful. Consorting with whores was sometimes even made to seem normal behavior.

Fragmentary remains of records from Babylon indicate that front-to-front copulation, with the woman on her back, was the normal position for sexual intercourse there. But they indicate also that variations on this sexual theme were not unknown. Those variations included anal entry, oral sex and homosexuality. The Old Testament (Genesis 38:9) describes the use of *coitus interruptus* for contraceptive purposes. (The biblical reference concerns Onan and the act of onanism was subsequently believed mistakenly to refer to masturbation.) Neither were "wet dreams" unknown in ancient times. According to a Babylonian maxim, if a man had a nocturnal emission while dreaming, he would face financial reverses; if, however, his erotic dream excited him enough so that he was awake when he ejaculated, he was destined to be wealthy and successful.

Various personal difficulties which are common now were known also in Babylonia. They include premature ejaculation and male impotence. In ancient times man's dominance over woman in sexual and other matters was unquestioned, suggesting that, contrary to a popular present day diagnosis, symbolic castration of the male by the "liberated" female is not at the root of these problems – at least it wasn't in Babylon.

Despite unabashed erotic display in religious worship in parts of the ancient world, puritanism in secular sexual matters began to emerge in communities increasingly governed by the formal rule of law. In Akkad, as in Babylon, this puritanism was closely related to the protection of property so that, for example, a man who deflowered another man's slave girl had to pay a stiff fine. In Babylon, a young man who seduced a girl, in effect robbing her father of some of his property, could be executed if he did not marry her. Joseph, in Egypt, realized how profoundly he would have transgressed against Potiphar and prevailing standards if he had succumbed to the pleas of Potiphar's wife that he bed her down.

But restrictions on sexuality went beyond questions of property rights. Questions of propriety arose. Around 2500 BC, Ipuwer, a sage of ancient Egypt, bemoaned the presence of "scented and overdressed young men and women [who] meet to adore the goddess of Love, to sing and enjoy themselves." In Assyria, men who engaged in homosexual acts were liable to be castrated. The Assyrian king, Tiglath-Pileser, was harsh with those who surrendered improperly to carnal temptations above their station. He ruled that, if a woman of his palace inadvertently exposed her private parts when attended by a messenger who was being instructed on an errand, and if that messenger then tarried with her rather than making off immediately, he was to be punished with one hundred lashes of the whip.

The Old Testament deprecated erotic display. Isaiah (3:16) condemned women who sought to excite men's carnal desires by walking "with stretched forth necks and wanton eyes, walking and mincing as they go. . . ." Elsewhere (Proverbs 6:25), men are warned to shun the temptations offered by beautiful women.

Wiles, stratagems and calculation were generally as widely

employed by females in pursuit of sexual attractiveness in the ancient world as they were to be in later times. Women rouged their cheeks with red ocher, tinted their fingernails and some-times dabbed their nipples with gold paint. Perfumes, per-fumed oils and eye shadow were liberally deployed. Skin care involved the application of various concoctions, including ostrich egg, bull's bile, antelope droppings and other exotic ingredients. Cow's blood was among substances employed to dye hair. Hairpins and headbands were used for coiffures.

An engraved pillar from ancient Egypt shows a young woman offering a king mandrake fruit, believed then to have aphrodisiac qualities and given the name "love apples." Among substances used by women as contraceptive pessaries were crocodile dung and gum preparations. Honey solutions were sometimes used for douching after copulation.

Home wall paintings of seductive dancing girls offended no moral standards in ancient Egypt. Erotic charms and amulets depicting copulating couples, penises and vulvas, were not uncommon there. Even death's threat to erotic fulfillment was limited in Egypt – miniature stone obelisks were constructed to house the penises of deceased men to ensure their virility in the afterlife.

Sex had been biologically instinctive for earliest humans. It then became a social force as well with primitive groups of men and women, setting the stage for the emergence of organized human society. In the ancient world, sexual fulfill-ment took on added dimensions. Erotic pleasure, deliberately pursued, became a factor in its own right, above and beyond blind instinctive compulsions, chance encounters and fertility rite charades. Also, romantic love came to be recognized as a factor in sexual motivation. As if to sanction this development, gods and goddesses of fertility often came to be worshipped as deities of love as well.

Poem from Ancient Mesopotamia

(Possibly recited by the priestess of the goddess of Love to the king
prior to ritual copulation.)

You have captivated me,
Let me stand tremblingly before you,
Bridegroom, take me to the bedchamber,
You have captivated me,
Let me stand tremblingly before you.
Lion, I would be taken by you to the bedchamber.

Bridegroom, let me caress you,
My precious caress is more savory than honey.
In the bedchamber, honey filled,
Let us enjoy your goodly beauty.
My precious caress is more savory than honey.

Egyptian love lyrics

Is there anything sweeter than this hour?
For I am with you, and you lift up my heart,
For is there not embracing and fondling when you visit me
And we give ourselves up to delights?
If you wish to caress my thigh,
Then I will offer you my breast also . . .
Would you leave because you wish something to drink?
Here, take my breasts.
They are full to overflowing and all for you . . .

Your love has gone all through my body
Like honey in water,
As a drug is mixed into spices,
As water is mingled with wine . . .

I go into the water to be with you
And come up again to you with a red fish
Lying so fine and splendid within my fingers
And I place it upon my breast . . .

From *The Song of Solomon*

She:
Your kisses engulf me;
Your love is more inebriating than wine;
You exude a tantalizing fragrance.
Your very name is enough to excite me;
No woman could resist you;
Take me away with you;
Be my king and take me to your chamber;
We will please each other there . . .

He:
How beautiful you are, my love;
How thrilling the pleasures you offer.
You are as stately as a palm tree;
Your breasts are as sweet as bunches of dates.
I will climb the tree and clutch its boughs;
Your breasts are like clusters of grapes.
Your breath has the perfume of apples;
The taste of you is like that of finest wine.

Men Like Gods

Men Like Gods

Do you pine for a sweet night of love,
For kisses without stop?
Then let's embrace and let us go
To bed, to bed, to bed.

— ARISTOPHANES, *Ecclesiazusae*

STANDARDS OF SEXUAL morality in ancient Greece have been an embarrassment to scholars over the ages. Until recent times (and often even now), men of learning tended to be straitlaced and exceedingly proper. It was not easy for many of them who idolized ancient Greek civilization to reconcile themselves to the fact that sexual pleasure and erotica were central themes in Greece. It has not been easy for them to accept that the incomparable Athenian orator Demosthenes went groveling to prostitutes and was humiliatingly overcharged for their services; that Sophocles, arguably the greatest tragic playwright of all time, loitered around the city walls trying to pick up pretty boys; that the statesman and general, Alcibiades, once a carefree homosexual, became a notorious womanizer ("Alcibiades, who was formerly no man, is now the man of all women"). Nor could they readily accept that the young priestesses of the Temple of Aphrodite in Corinth, whose prayers were deemed particularly important at times of national calamity, were famous for their sexual skills; that the Greek word for "orgy" referred originally to certain forms of religious ritual (the term did not acquire immoral overtones until Christian times); that naked boys and girls customarily engaged in organized wrestling matches in Sparta. Even so committed an admirer of ancient Greece as the Victorian historian W.E.H. Lecky, author of the monumental *History of European Morals*, felt obliged to confess that there were aspects of Greek life which he found "eminently unpleasing."

Nor could honest scholars dismiss those "unpleasing" aspects as trivial or uncharacteristic. We know more about ancient Greece than about anything that came before. The vices, virtues, customs and quirks of its people are well documented. Records of their moods and motivations have been handed down reasonably intact. The personalities of ancient Greece – political leaders, philosophers, courtesans, social climbers, quacks – are identifiable by name, reputation and achievement. The Greeks compiled a comprehensive, enduring record of what they thought and did. Their life-styles are known to us.

The picture that emerges is of a people who were self-important, introspective, pretentious, logical, sometimes somber, sometimes frivolous, always questing. The Greeks were the world's first individualists. They inhabited an area of contending schools of philosophical thought, of conflicting concepts of "the good life," of "hidden harmonies" and logical conundrums. As for sexual pleasure, they lived in an atmosphere which casually countenanced public erotic display and where carnal satisfaction was deemed a prize eminently worth pursuing.

Pericles, the most illustrious political leader Greece ever produced, the man after whom the golden Periclean age was named, lived openly and happily with the best-known courtesan of his time. Symposiums in ancient Greece, gatherings famous throughout history for their scintillating intellectual give-and-take, were often punctuated with group sex. Hippocrates, the "father of medicine," was the first (of many in history) to suggest that sexual indulgence was essential to save women (only) from insanity. Erotic pursuits and pastimes were constituent elements of the cultural climate of this cradle of western moral and political ideas and ideals.

Among the galaxy of gods and goddesses who crowded the

Greek pantheon of deities were a host of lecherous immortals who pointed the way to a form of ribaldry and sexual mischief that had been totally absent from earlier, more earnest erotic moods, legends and tales. Just as in later ages *The Lives of the Saints* would promote virtuous and charitable behavior, their libertine antics nourished and encouraged popular approval for uninhibited sexual pleasure in a culture where prostitution became as conventional as marriage (and as class-stratified as society itself).

Disenchanted citizens did not disfigure the faces of statues of gods which were everywhere in Athens; they broke off the erect phalluses with which many of those statues were adorned. A rash of such castrations at times of national crisis was taken as an omen of impending disaster.

Vases, cups, lamps, doors, gates and various household gewgaws were adorned with scenes of copulation, sexual play and other erotic imagery. Reputable artists were commissioned to produce such objects for well-ordered households. The ancient Greeks saw nothing unusual or remarkable about that – they considered sexual arousal and sexual appetites to be normal and healthy and, incidentally, not necessarily associated with romantic love.

Theater, which had its genesis in ancient Greece, was by tradition liberally sprinkled there with erotic references and byplay. Eminent playwrights wrote lines for the stage in Athens as bawdy as any ever conceived. Foremost among them was Aristophanes whose most enduring comedy, *Lysistrata*, tells of women who vow to withhold sex from their soldier husbands to encourage them to end the war they are fighting. One of the play's more memorable scenes involves Athenians pretending to believe suspiciously that sex-hungry Spartans, arriving with penises erect for peace negotiations, are hiding spears under their cloaks.

Greek audiences responded with glee to the salacious lines with which Aristophanes dotted his comedies. "If you keep pestering me, I'll lift both your legs and stick it right between them" (from *The Birds*), and "I am primed, made stiff for love by the nudge of a friendly bosom!" (from *The Archanians*).

Male actors in bawdy comedies sometimes wore artificial penises strapped round their waists to heighten sexual farce. Females engaged in highly suggestive dancing and prancing and were often involved in sexual byplay on the stage.

In its earliest form, Greek erotica was religious, focusing on the sex lives of the gods. Mount Olympus, where the gods lived and romped, was depicted as an ethereal Peyton Place for immortals, a realm of – among other things – seemingly endless hanky-panky, seduction and rape. The supreme god, Zeus, ravisher of countless females, both immortal and mortal, served as a model. His erotic exploits gave rise to a rich catalogue of legends. In one such legend, he turned himself into a bull to rape the Earth goddess, Demeter. In another, he transformed himself into a swan to seduce Leda, Queen of Sparta. He pursued and overcame Metis, goddess of wisdom, despite the many disguises she adopted, and then swallowed her whole because of the prophecy that their offspring would depose him. Ironically, among Zeus's duties as a god was guardian of the sanctity of marriage.

He was, however, far from unique among the Greek deities in matters related to the range of sexual diversion. Poseidon, god of the sea, was also known for the determination with which he indulged in seduction and rape. To escape his insistent advances, Demeter – repeatedly plowed and planted by other gods as only an Earth goddess could be – turned herself into a mare, only to find that Poseidon had taken the form of a stallion the better to mount her. Like other Olympians, the sea god repeatedly resorted to quick-change artistry, at his disposal by virtue of his divine nature, to assume disguises and shapes best suited for particular sexual conquests – sometimes a bird, sometimes a ram – whatever the situation required.

Poseidon's wife, Amphitrite, employed a related skill for other purposes. Angered by her husband's flirtations with the nymph, Scylla, she transformed Scylla into a monster with six heads, twelve feet and a bark. Another of the objects of Poseidon's desire also suffered cruelly because of it. He seduced Medusa in the temple of the goddess Athena. Athena was so offended by this sacrilege that she turned Medusa's hair into snakes.

Apollo, the god of music and poetry, was sufficiently hand-some, graceful and charming not to require undignified sub-terfuges in making sexual conquests. But despite his attrac-tions, those he sought to seduce sometimes rejected his atten-tions – strangely, in view of the license such legends usually portrayed. In one tale, Daphne, daughter of the river god, declined his overtures, escaped by being swallowed into the Earth and reappeared as a laurel tree. Spurned, but display-ing a graciousness rare among the Olympians, Apollo decreed that the laurel tree would from then on be sacred. Less charit-able were his dealings with Cassandra, daughter of the king of Troy. In return for her promise to lie with him, Apollo granted her the gift of prophecy. When Cassandra then refused to fulfill her part of the deal, Apollo begged her for just one kiss, breathed deeply into her mouth and deprived her of the powers of persuasion. From then on, Cassandra could foretell the future but no one believed her.

Aphrodite, goddess of beauty and love, was the *femme fatale* among the deities. She tormented her fellow gods with her loveliness, arousing their desire, rivalry and jealousy. If Greek poets were to be believed, she was blessed with an incompar-ably seductive sweet mouth, firm bosom, gleaming eyes and delicate neck. Even her magnificently formed posterior was glorified by Greek sculptors who dedicated statues to the goddess "with the tantilizing buttocks." Teased by her beauty, Zeus made Aphrodite susceptible to the attractions of mortal men. She was subsequently entwined in a series of brief erotic adventures with mere mortals though, like Zeus, she was supposed to be the divine protectress of the sanctity of mar-riage. This may partly account for the derision widely directed against matrimony in ancient Greece.

Like many peoples emerging from prehistory in other places, the earliest known inhabitants of Greece indulged in erotic fertility rites. Dionysus was a fertility god probably borrowed from peoples to the north. He was originally known to the Greeks in idol form simply as an erect phallus. His rites included drunken orgies, displays of huge wooden phalluses and sexual charades which were the origin of western theater. His retinue included mischievous satyrs and playful nymphs, both noted for their sexual revelry. Equally mischievous were the gods Pan and Priapus, often included in the retinue of Dionysus. Priapus, sometimes considered Dionysus's son, was invariably represented with penis erect. Lucky charms exhibited him that way.

The catalogue of erotically-inclined Greek deities is inexhaustible – Eos, goddess of the dawn, who was inclined to force her attractions on beautiful young men; Ares, the god of war, who briefly won the love of the incomparable Aphrodite; Selene, the moon goddess, who bore the mighty Zeus a love child – the list goes on and on.

Deploying their gods and goddesses in increasingly sophisticated erotic legends was a convenient device for city-dwelling Greeks, who were still a minority in their largely agrarian land. They adapted earthy countryside erotica (fertility festivals in fields and groves) to more advanced art forms and sophisticated mythical substance. Dionysus and his nymphs and satyrs still made their sexual rounds in the countryside. But their hayseed gaucheries, though quaint, could be too coarse for the proud citizens of the city-states, who were excessively aware of their cultivated, elegant tastes. For many of them, Dionysian urges and ecstasies conveniently became symbolic of a new religious experience, a transcendental link with the divine. For others, the more polished behavior and attitudes of other Olympians helped maintain the credibility of the deities.

Nevertheless, confining erotica to those deities wore thin as Greek civilization grew more refined. It wasn't a question of changes in human sexual standards and behavior; it was how erotic performance should properly be displayed in art and literature. If gods – with goddesses and nymphs at their disposal – often chose to dally with mortal females in living legend, there seemed little reason why mortal men couldn't make a public virtue of doing the same. Glorification of erotic antics was thus gradually and painlessly extended to humans who could then openly proclaim their sexual desires and pleasures without feeling the need to use religious observance as justification. It was in Greece that sexual display became truly secularized for the first time.

Pandora, according to Greek legend the first mortal woman, was created by command of Zeus as vengeance against mortal men who had offended him. "I will give men . . . an evil thing in which they may all be glad at heart while they embrace their destruction." The source of man's misery, Pandora was endowed with deceit as well as beauty, mischief as well as charm. Given a vase ("Pandora's box") by the gods but forbidden to open it, she proceeded to lift the lid, thereby releasing all the troubles that have plagued mankind ever since.

Judging by the Greek male's attitude toward matrimony, the urge to marry was one of those plagues. Prompted by the availability of dowries and/or the desire to perpetuate their lineage, men took wives. But it was with the firm understanding that their spouses would serve only two functions – keeping house and bearing children. In Sparta, a woman's name was engraved on her tomb only if she died in childbirth. The philosopher Theophrastus moaned, "To support a poor wife is hard; to put up with a rich one is torture." The lives of marriageable girls and married women were sharply confined and their horizons were narrowly restricted. The story was told of a man who, informed by his friends that his breath always smelled foul, rebuked his wife for not having told him. She innocently replied, "I thought all men smelled like that."

On the Greek stage, young men were depicted as falling in love with courtesans rather than with girls they hoped to marry. Marriage was represented as a duty, often an unpleasant one. The poet Theognis compared married life with cattle breeding. Much was made in the theater and in poetry of the drudges and scolds wives were commonly assumed to be. Even Hera, the supreme goddess, was an insufferable nuisance to her husband, Zeus. The poet Hipponax was much quoted for having said, "There are only two days in life when a wife pleases her husband – on the day he marries her and on the day he buries her." Few were surprised when the illustrious Socrates, condemned to be poisoned for having corrupted the youth of Athens with wayward wisdom, ordered that his wife, Xanthippe, reputed to be an impossible nag, not be allowed anyway near his death bed.

Prevailing attitudes made a mockery of romantic legends in which, for example, Odysseus and Penelope shared a profound and undying matrimonial love or in which the Trojan War could be launched to retrieve Menelaus's wife, the exquisite Helen.

Marriage came to be held in such disrepute in ancient Greece that Solon, the great Athenian lawgiver, contemplated making it compulsory to save society from complete disruption. In fact, laws were passed reserving certain important state offices for married men in the hope that being married would lose some of its stigma. Nevertheless, men turned elsewhere for their erotic pleasures – to prostitutes, to the wives of other men, to homosexuality.

Demosthenes said, "We marry wives to produce our children and look after our homes. We take concubines for day-to-day services. We go to prostitutes for pleasure." Neglected, bored, largely unneeded, unfulfilled by dildoes which (made by cobblers) gradually became available, many wives also cast about for extramarital encounters. To save their virtue (more likely to save the honor of their husbands), Solon established official secular prostitution for the first time. Seeking to direct the sexual urges of men away from the wives of other men, he set up a large, state-controlled, low-priced brothel in Athens in the sixth century BC (it was the first of many there) and used the proceeds to build a temple. It was dedicated, appropriately, to Aphrodite, goddess of love.

The services of prostitutes were considered so commendable that young men who still turned to liaisons with married women instead were thought foolish by their elders. The writer Xenarchus said, ". . . there are pretty girls in the brothels. You can see them with their breasts bared, exhibiting themselves. . . . You can choose whichever takes your fancy, slender or fat, big or small. . . . You don't have to get a ladder and creep sneakily along, crawling through the chimney or smuggled in wrapped in a bale of straw. In the brothels, the girls make the advances. They call you daddy if you're getting on in years, or big boy if you're still a kid. . . . And it doesn't cost much."

A three-level stratification of prostitution in ancient Greece was established and meticulously maintained. At the lowest level, common whores either received their clients in brothels or walked the streets. Many of the street walkers, particularly numerous in sea ports, performed their services in convenient recesses of dark back streets. The door posts of brothels were adorned with painted or carved phalluses, for identification purposes. Whores were forbidden to circulate outside brothels except well into the evening when they were unlikely to encounter and embarrass respectable matrons in the streets. On these excursions, they were required to dress distinctively (in some places, they had to wear yellow wigs) so as to be readily identifiable. But, though barely more than slaves, they were not considered pariahs. Rather, they were thought of as a form of public servant of low rank but valuable function. They were cheap and available to all men.

More expensive and more exclusive were call girls – commonly known as "flute girls" – who, aside from their erotic proficiencies, could play musical instruments, dance or juggle. They were usually commissioned to attend private parties, banquets, symposiums and other gatherings at which they entertained assembled guests before pairing-off or before orgies took place, though they sometimes performed oral sex with guests in the course of the proceedings. The profession of these girls was, nevertheless, considered respectable and they sometimes displayed their artistic skills at public festivals where crowds, drawn by their reputations for non-sexual accomplishments, came to see them dance or hear them play music. There is no equivalent for this kind of call girl today – a comparison would exist if highly successful, famous female pop music stars could be booked to sing at parties and then sexually satisfy the male guests.

Most distinguished and respected among the Greek prostitutes were the *hetaerai*. These were courtesans who, in addition to being extremely well versed in the ways of sexual arousal and fulfillment, could boast of great beauty, intelligence and wit. They were maintained in luxurious quarters by their client or clients, or maintained comfortable quarters of their own where they received visitors who could afford their expensive talents. They were much acclaimed in the writings of the period:

> If one of us happens to come in feeling gloomy, she greets him with pleasant teasing, kisses him, not clutching her lips tightly together as if he were a nuisance but opening wide her mouth like a baby bird . . . drawing off his gloom and making him jolly again.
>
> EPHIPPUS

Hetaerai who established enduring liaisons with prominent personalities were better known publicly than the wives of those men. And while wives were almost invariably the butt of jokes and jibes whenever mentioned in Greek literature, hetaerai were invariably depicted as remarkable women, irresistibly charming, talented and stunning – or profoundly wicked as only formidable personages could be.

Hetaerai were asked by famous sculptors to pose for statues of goddesses and many of the magnificent figures found today in museums were molded in their images. At a court trial in which Phryne of Thespiae, a celebrated hetaera, was accused of sacrilege, her counsel drew off her tunic and so dazzled the court with her naked beauty that she was acquitted. The verdict was that no one so lovely could have offended the gods.

Aspasia, the hetaera who became the mistress of Pericles, was probably the only courtesan in history openly recognized as a major national figure in her own right. Many of Pericles's much-acclaimed speeches were said to have been inspired by Aspasia's ideas and conversation. Another hetaera, Thais, was mistress of Alexander the Great and later became queen of Egypt. Thais was said to have been so beautiful that "the whole of Greece had at some time languished before her door."

Many plays were written around the theme of men lusting after beautiful hetaerai; a recurring refrain concerned father and son competing for the same hetaera's favors. In Greek Alexandria, the most lavish villas were identifiable by the name of the hetaerai who lived in them or for whom they had been built. Statues of the more celebrated hetaerai were erected next to those of statesmen and generals in public buildings.

Despite the political skills and intellectual capacities displayed by some courtesans, their fame and success depended primarily on their beauty. The ancient Greeks were obsessed with the magnificence of beauty – beauty in form, beauty in content, beauty in design. Beauty was a quality by which they could measure virtually all things. Nevertheless, the golden-haired Adonis and fair Greek female beauty were primarily idealized inventions. Most Greeks at the time did not look much different from most Greeks today, with a prevalence of dark-haired, dark-complexioned people. But cosmetics were liberally applied and various substances and implements were used to enhance feminine looks. These included rouge, seaweed paint, white lead, beauty plasters, wigs, hairnets, earrings and bracelets. Breast girdles and bands for bracing up bosoms were used – in *The Iliad*, Hera, seeking to charm Zeus, asks to borrow Aphrodite's "magic girdle of love and longing, which subdues the hearts of all the gods and mortal dwellers upon Earth." Aphrodite agrees to lend it and "loosed from her bosom the broidered girdle, wherein are fashioned all manner of allurements. . . ."

The sap of a mallow plant was believed capable of exciting sexual passion, particularly of women. More popular aphrodisiacs were onions, snails and crabmeat. Sexual potency could be increased by wearing the right testicle of an ass in an amulet. The same effect could be derived from placing some wormwood under the bed or eating pith of the pomegranate tree. (The menstrual discharge of a woman menstruating for the first time after loss of her virginity could be dabbed on door posts to make houses invulnerable to evil spells.)

A variety of superstitions were invoked for contraceptive purposes. It was believed, for example, that if a woman held a certain kind of pebble in her hand while copulating, she would not conceive.

To enhance their beauty, women plucked out or shaved off their pubic hair. Perfumes, notably those made of violet and wild thyme, and fragrant oils were very popular and often employed to excess, not only by women. Solon felt called upon to ban the sale of fragrant oils to men in Athens, although a thorough pre-copulation oiling of the body was commonly prescribed.

Beauty, the search for beauty and its appreciation were persistent themes in Greek life. At festivals of Dionysus, naked youths and young women exposed their beauty for all to admire. In historical legend, Menelaus readily forgave war-causing Helen's adultery when he again saw her bare, beautiful breasts. Everyone was moved by the story of Pygmalion, the king of Cyprus, who was said to have fallen in love with an exquisite statute of Aphrodite and took it to bed with him. Nor were eyebrows raised when word spread through Athens that a man had been so smitten by another statue of the goddess of love that he had embraced it, leaving a stain on its stone flanks.

Though the Greeks easily adjusted to alien components of beauty (blond hair, fair complexions), conventional elements of the female form often jarred against their ideals of beauty and grace, as defined by their artists and poets. Full breasts, wide hips and voluptuous curves, which earlier (and later) caused erotic arousal, contrasted hopelessly with the boyish, trim, slender human lines they favored.

Greek literature is full of references to "beautiful boys" who dazzled and captivated even mature, distinguished men. The youthful, naked male figure was the subject to which Greek sculptors most readily turned. Similarly, vase painters (an honored profession and skill) regularly decorated vessels with masterful images of naked athletes and warriors and when, later, naked female figures also began appearing on vases, they tended to be boyish in shape.

Philosophers and poets sought to elevate boy-love into an incomparable expression of the majesty of human feeling. It was, they contended, purer and more aesthetically satisfying than a man's love for a woman. Plato described how a roomful of grown men grew awkward and confused when a pretty boy entered. Men competed for the favors of beautiful boys – and paid heavily for them. Boys flirted with men in market places and men went there to find young lovers.

Sexual relations between grown men was not uncommon in Greece. It was claimed by some that such relations improved the character of the individuals involved in a way that love between a man and a woman could not. The Sacred Band of Thebes, a unit of elite fighting men, consisted exclusively of homosexual pairs. The assumption was that they would fight gloriously for each other in battle, as well as for Thebes. But the ideal object of homosexual pursuit in Athens and other Greek city-states was a beautiful boy – a "fresh-faced kid," before he became a "shaggy goat."

Boy prostitutes were available to men, though those who saw boy-love as the purest form of love were deeply disappointed that a price should be placed on it. The rape of youths was often part of in-group initiation ceremonies. This took place on hunting excursions, for example, and in gymnasiums.

Homosexuality did not necessarily exclude heterosexual love. Greek men who engaged in sexual relations with youths often copulated with women as well. Indeed, there was a running debate between bisexuals in Athens as to which – male or female lovers – were to be preferred. The poet Dioscorides, known for his praise of boy-love, was also able to write:

> *They drive me mad, her rosy lips,*
> *Wherefrom my soul its nectar sips,*
> *Her eyes a liquid radiance dart*
> *Traps to ensnare my fluttering heart,*
> *Her breasts, twin sisters firmly grown,*
> *Two hills that love their master own . . .*

Bisexual conduct was sanctioned and promoted by various legends. The eminently masculine Zeus dallied as well with the boy, Ganymede, cup bearer of the gods. In Cyprus, a male-female divinity was worshiped and, in tribute to it, a young man was chosen each year to lie on a bed and imitate the contortions of a woman in childbirth.

There was also the legend of Hermaphroditus, a boy of great beauty, whose looks captivated the water nymph, Salmacis. She lured him into her pond, lay with him and, wishing never to be parted from him, had the gods unite them forever into a single being, having both sexes. Legend further had it that any man who bathed in the nymph's pond emerged effeminate, half-man, half-woman.

Despite the reputation Greek civilization developed for widespread homosexuality, it was, in fact, largely confined to members of the intellectual elite, to the aristocracy and, to a lesser extent, to the military and athletes. The population as a whole tended to think of homosexuals as either exotic or comic figures, eccentric, hoity-toity or foppish. Aristophanes reflected prevailing attitudes when he poked fun at one of his characters who wanted to live in a place where "the father of a pretty boy" would rebuke him because, "You meet my son as he comes out of the gym, fresh from his bath, but you don't kiss him, you don't hug him, you don't fondle his testicles! Do you call that being a friend?"

Lesbian love was not practiced, at least not overtly, in the overwhelmingly male-oriented Greek society. What remains of the poetry of Sappho is rich in expressions of love for other females ("I need but see you for my words to stumble and my voice to falter" she wrote of the mesmerizing effect one of them had on her). She founded a school for young women on the island of Lesbos, hence the name "lesbian." But, despite subsequent legend, there was nothing at the time to indicate that her love for other women, though profound, was anything other than what would later be called platonic. Indeed, one legend was that she committed suicide, jumping to her death from a cliff, because of unrequited love for a man. Whatever the truth, Sappho's expressions of love for women initiated the poetry of romantic love in the western world and the depth of feeling in her verse inspired many later poets.

Despite the prominence of sexuality in ancient Greece, Greek civilization produced the earliest philosophical doubts about the value and justification of sexual pleasure. In their ceaseless probings, the Greeks devised a separation between body and soul that was to haunt and muddle western thought from that point on.

Plato was the most prominent of the Greek philosophers who counseled that the soul was superior to the body and that sexual desire was debasing in that it reduced potentially noble humans to the level of animals. He considered copulation so bestially repulsive that it was proper to indulge in it only in privacy or in the dark. And Democritus, who proclaimed that pleasure was a supreme goal for humans, emphasized that he meant pleasures of the mind because pleasures of the senses were, he said, brief, ultimately distressing and to be studiously avoided.

It is easy to see how such philosophy could readily graduate into a rationale for homosexual indulgence. If men were to shun the carnal delights offered by women, they would shun women altogether for fear of being led astray during weak moments. Seeking contentments and pleasures of male companionship and the higher love it could provide, many discovered that this higher love came equipped with sensual pleasures of a different category, no less overpowering to the senses than the heterosexual joys they meticulously avoided for philosophical reasons.

Others, however, did indeed find platonic relationships with others and the ethereal, non-sexual pleasures they sought in such companionship – at least they continued to pursue those goals with unrelenting perseverance. In the process, they laid the groundwork for feelings of guilt and sin about sexual pleasure that were later to plague and confound the human psyche. They were heralds of the warm, gratifying, comforting "soul-mate" type of chaste romanticism that was often to add complicating dimensions to male-female relations (and still does). They set the stage for an abhorrence of sex that was to feature so prominently during medieval and Victorian times.

Methods employed by prostitutes in ancient Greece to enhance their attractions.

. . . suppose one girl is too small: a cork sole is stitched into her dainty shoes. Another is too tall: she wears a thin slipper and cocks her head to one side when she walks abroad. This reduces her height. One has no hips: she sews together a bustle and puts it on beneath her dress so that all who catch sight of the fine curves of her back cry out in applause. One has a stomach that is too fat: such have bosoms made of the stuff comic actors use, padding themselves straight out in such fashion, they then pull forward, as with punting-poles, the covering of their stomachs. Another woman has eyebrows too light: they paint them with lamp-black. Still another . . . is too dark: she plasters herself over with white lead. One has a complexion too white: she rubs on rouge. A part of one's body is beautiful: this part she displays bare. She has pretty teeth: she must, of course, laugh . . .

—FROM *The Wise Men at Dinner* BY ATHENAEUS

From *The Dialogues* of Lucian

"Jupiter's Warning To Cupid"

CUPID: I beg your pardon if I have done you wrong. I am only a child.

JUPITER: Just because you have neither a beard nor a grey hair in your head ? You're as old as the hills and full of mischief . . . Is it child's play, you clumsy dolt, that for your own perversity and pleasure, you've made me into all sorts of things ? Because of you not a single mortal likes me at all, leaving me with nothing but magic to use against them. I have to turn myself into a satyr, a bull, and eagle, even a shower of gold to get near a mortal woman. And what do I get out of it? They love the bull or the swan, but are frightened stiff when I appear in my real shape.

CUPID: That's understandable. How could mortals bear the sight of mighty Jupiter . . . If you want to be loved, you'd better lay aside your lightening bolt and that huge shield of yours. Comb your hair . . . Let pipes and drums announce your arrival.

JUPITER: You can keep that kind of advice. I don't want to be agreeable if that's the price to pay . . . Hard or easy, I won't renounce the joy of love. But I insist that it be less troublesome in the future. Your job is to arrange it. That is why I pardon you this time.

(Though Greek, Lucian lived during the time of the Roman Empire and therefore used the Roman names, Jupiter and Cupid, rather than their Greek equivalents, Zeus and Eros.)

From a letter from the flute girl Megara to the hetaera Bacchis about the happenings at a banquet.

. . . in the midst of it all, an argument developed which livened things up. It was over whether Thryallis or Myrrhine was more beautiful. Myrrhine dropped her girdle. Her gown was transparent. She whirled and it seemed that what we gazed on was lilies through crystal. She gave her hips a precipitate motion, glancing down all the while at her voluptuous masses of flesh which she was shaking. Then . . . she began murmuring something or other in a low moaning voice which still thrills me to think of it. But Thryallis did not yield the victory. She came forward . . . and let fall her garments, displaying . . . her rival charms. "Look," she cooed . . . "at the fall of my hips, at the fineness and whiteness of my skin, and at those rose-pink leaves which the hand of pleasure itself seems to have scattered over the lovely contours of my body . . . Those spheres of mine do not tremble the way Myrrhine's do. Instead their movement is like the gentle murmuring of a wave." Saying those words, she redoubled her lascivious quiverings, displaying so much agility that a burst of applause arose, giving her triumphal honors.

From *The Symposium* **of Plato (427-347 BC)**

Pausanias speaks :
. . . there are two Aphrodites . . . There can be no doubt of the common nature of the love which is associated with the Common Aphrodite. It is random and arbitrary and the kind of love sought after by the baser kind of man. Its characteristics are, first, that it is aimed at women quite as much as young men. Second, in either case, it is simply physical rather than spiritual. Third, this sort of love prefers its object to be as stupid as possible because its only aim is satisfaction of physical desires and it is not overly concerned with the way this is accomplished. . . . But the Heavenly Aphrodite with which the other love is associated has no female aspect but arises totally from the male. It is free of base wantonness. Hence those inspired by this form of love are drawn toward the male sex and value it as being naturally more sturdy and more intelligent.

Simplicity
Confounded

Simplicity Confounded

When you find the spot where a woman loves to be touched, don't be too shy to touch it. . . . You'll see her eyes sparkle. . . . She'll moan and whisper sweet nothings and sigh contentedly. . . . But be careful that you don't gallop ahead, leaving her behind. And make sure also that she doesn't reach the finish before you do.

— OVID, *The Art of Love*

THE ATTITUDE OF the Romans toward sex was precise and practical – not unlike their approach to building their famous roads. Just as all roads led to Rome, so all sexual indulgence was meant to lead to nothing more nor less than unembellished physical pleasure. Unlike the Greeks, who were addicted to philosophizing about everything, the Romans felt no need to glorify sexual satisfaction or to find in it things that, for them, simply weren't there.

Several emperors may have indulged in bizarre erotic sexual pastimes. Because of the city's dramatic end, the ruins of Pompeii boast the telltale remains of the most famous whorehouse in history. As elsewhere in the ancient world, various religious festivals were marked by orgiastic revelry. But the Romans made few efforts to complicate carnal satisfaction with a search for beauty, grace or depth of feeling, or to cloak it with intellectual folderol. The poet Horace, who was to become a strong advocate of traditional, sober Roman virtues, was precise about that:

> *When you're feeling randy,*
> *If a girl or boy is handy,*

Attack at once!
Or would you rather suffer in silence?
Not me!
I like love fast and easy.

Architects of the most elaborate empire the world had ever known, lawgivers extraordinary, magnificent warriors, creators of a sprawling network of trade routes, the Romans were direct, down-to-earth and generally unimaginative when it came to erotic pursuits (until influences of the eastern regions they ruled unhinged their sense of propriety and broadened their erotic horizons).

Ovid, who compiled the first known sex guide and handbook, was eminently practical and explicit in his approach. ("If she's wearing something seductive, tell her, 'You excite me!' " "Use force. Women like forceful men. They often seem to surrender unwillingly when they're really anxious to give in.") In proffering such advice, Ovid shied meticulously clear of romantic sentiments. The poet Catullus did try to frame his sexual exploits in a romantic setting and ended up a cynic. (". . . the anguish which cunning Venus inflicted on me; how she shattered my life and how I burned like Etna. . . .") There were other written expressions of such volcanic passion, but they were the exception in Rome where sexual indulgence was generally uncomplicated and the emotional extravagances of romantic love were often thought to be unseemly and a little foolish.

Even after the Romans had already bestowed upon vast, previously uncitified regions the now dubious gift of organized urban life, they themselves were playfully partaking in ribald celebrations no more sophisticated than a roll in the hay. The Liberalia in March, in honor of the god of fertility, and the Saturnalia in December (later to make way for Christmas), in honor of the harvest god, were occasions marked by much sexual revelry. During the Liberalia, huge effigies of the male genitals were loaded onto wagons, displayed around the countryside and then carried through the cities. These displays were still going on during the later period of the Roman Empire and aroused the outrage of St. Augustine who scorned those who "exulted in such beastliness." Bacchanalias, in honor of the god of wine and revelry, had been officially banned long before, not because they were licentious but because they had grown unruly, marked by "noises and shrieks which resound through the city all night."

A number of moralistic voices were raised in protest against prevailing attitudes. The historian Tacitus wrote admiringly of Germanic tribes to the north where unvirtuous women had their hair cut off and were publicly whipped. The philosopher Lucretius complained that sexual activity promoted irrational behavior and drained the energies of participants. The playwright Seneca objected to the flirtatious attire some women affected:

> I see silken clothes, if they can be called clothes, which protect neither a woman's body nor her modesty, and in which she cannot honestly declare that she is not stark naked. These garments are bought for great amounts of money from peoples unknown to us in the normal course of trade. Why? So that Roman women may show as much of themselves to everybody as they display before their lovers in the bedroom.

Public ribaldry was frowned upon. Though neither taboo nor forbidden, it was uncouth. But to have advocated chastity for reasons of moral purity would have struck most Romans as fuddy-duddy and contrary to natural behavior.

Cato the Censor, a stern puritan who once had a man expelled from the Senate for kissing his wife in front of their daughter (he believed such intimacies should be private), was not averse to nocturnal visits from his comely slave girl. The poet Martial noted, "I have searched through the entire city for a girl who would say *no*; there is no such female!" Trinkets in the form of phalluses, some with small bells affixed to them, were worn as talismans. Phallus-shaped statuary adorned many a home and elaborate mosaics representing male genitals could be found on floors of the villas of many wealthy Romans. Some Roman citizens chose to masquerade their indulgences behind proud claims that they were perpetuating earthy, venerable peasant virtues which, they said, had originally made Rome great.

Cicero, clearly in the mainstream of Roman thought, sharply challenged the more extreme of the puritans: "If there is anyone who thinks that young men should be forbidden to make love, even to prostitutes, he is certainly a man of stern righteousness. . . . He is, however, out of touch not only with what is happening today but even with the ways of our fathers. For when was it not customary?"

Unlike ancient Greece, where wives tended to be incidental to the day-to-day lives of their husbands, matrimonial bonds were at first strong and meaningful in Rome. The wife – a "mama" figure extraordinary – was a stabilizing factor in the family and was prized in a way that Greek husbands would never have comprehended. In traditional wedding ceremonies, the husband pretended to drag the wife away from her mother – probably a throwback to primitive "marriage by capture." But though his wife was mistress of his home, the husband had complete authority over her and their children, both by law and practice. He could divorce her for unseemly behavior, which might mean simply drinking wine, and he could kill her for committing adultery, without fear of legal consequences. He himself could be severely punished for adultery, but only if he committed it with another married woman.

During the later days of the Roman republic, however, a transformation took place in the status of women. It may have resulted from improved education of girls or the influence of Greece and other permissive cultures to the East to which Rome was exposed as a result of the enormous inflow of peoples from all corners of its realm. Women acquired greater legal rights, including the right to own and administer property. They began increasingly to assert themselves and were less and less committed to spending their days within their homes, exclusively concerned with the well-being of their husbands and children. Cato moaned that neither shame nor the authority of their husbands was keeping women at home any longer. He warned the men of Rome that "the moment women have attained equality with you, they will have become your superiors. . . . Women," he said, "are violent and uncontrollable creatures. You can't give them the reins and not expect them to kick over the traces."

Nevertheless, sexual equality was never attained, much less female superiority. Men remained unquestionably and overwhelmingly dominant in Roman society. However, some restraints on female behavior were loosened. Contraception and abortion, unthinkable to respectable matrons in old Rome, became increasingly popular. Many of the recommended contraceptive methods and devices were pure mumbo-jumbo. A woman was advised to wear the liver of a cat in a container attached to her left foot to avoid conception, or to hold her breath at the moment of sexual climax, or to squat or sneeze soon afterward. If she spat three times into the mouth of a frog, she would not conceive for a year. She could avoid conception by extracting a certain substance from a spider, wrapping it in a patch of deer skin and applying the package to her skin just before dawn. Other methods may have been more effective, including the use of honey and oils to block the uterine passage.

Rigid standards of sexual morality were considered laughably inadequate. Horace, no doubt stretching facts a bit, bemoaned the change and vividly described new attitudes :

> *Each ripe female knows now how to traipse through*
> *Bouncy Greek dances. She also has shameful skills*
> *And is always ready*
> *To throw herself into lewd love affairs.*
> *She seeks younger men*
> *When her husband's out drinking and gives*
> *Any stud forbidden favors*
> *On the double in a back room.*
> *She even answers enthusiastically*
> *When pedlars call or roving seamen*
> *Make their pitch.*

Upper-class women increasingly sought sexual adventures outside the home. The poet Propertius said it had reached a stage whereby fidelity in a Roman matron was so rare that it was worthy of special praise. What would formerly have been deemed immodest appearance became fashionable. Women dyed their hair and grew addicted to fussy hairdos to make themselves more attractive on their once rare but now frequent perambulations. They took to ever more complicated arrays of cosmetics, including soot for eye shadow, white lead, rouge and something produced from an extract of crocodile dung (used as a mud pack).

Such beauty aids and artifices drew snide comments from moralists. One observer commented wryly:

> If you saw a woman getting out of bed in the morning, you would find her as repulsive as a monkey. That's why she shuts herself up in her room and shuns the company of men until she's ready for them. Servant girls as wretched looking as she is wait on her, plastering her miserable face with all kinds of cosmetics. A woman doesn't just splash some cold water on her face to wake up. No. A steady flow of concoctions and salves are deployed to touch up her complexion. A parade of servants forms up, each with something else: a jug; a mirror; a collection of jars, enough to stock a pharmacy ; boxes full of mischief; tooth powders and stuff to blacken her eyelids.

Juvenal, never gentle in his comments about women, added his derision:

> *Every month she rejuvenates her face,*
> *During which it is coated with grease.*
> *That's her husband's time to claim his right.*
> *He tries to kiss her and gets stuck in glue.*
> *But when she meets her lover,*
> *She's straight from her bath, twinkling bright.*
> *For him her mouth is fresh and sweetened,*
> *Her body delicately oiled.*

69

No matter how haggard she looks at home,
The change is miraculous.
Her face is renewed, refreshed, restored.
The crust is removed. Her cheeks are silky smooth,
Polished with a wash of ass's milk.

As the old order disintegrated, divorce became common, bachelorhood became fashionable and, as the historian E.O. James pointed out, "With the breakup of family life, a marked decline set in from the high standard of female virtue maintained in the earlier period." This was particularly noticeable among the upper classes. For men, living with a concubine rather than a wife came to be seen as an ideal arrangement. Juvenal asked waspishly why any man would endure the "tyranny of a bitch" when a rope was available to end his misery. Cicero, no philanderer, complained that he had difficulty coping with both philosophy and a wife at the same time.

Ironically, among Cicero's many eloquent public performances was a diatribe against a loose-living woman. It came during his defense of a man who was accused of various vile crimes merely because, Cicero claimed, he had presumed to spurn the woman's advances. He said that the woman, Clodia, once the object of Catullus's passionate poetry, was a "lady friend to everybody," that she lived like a harlot, ridden with lust and vice. She was, said Cicero, a woman who, "with her manner of dress and her gait . . . by her disreputable looks and loose language, by embracing and kissing men, acts like a lewd and wanton whore." His eloquence won the day in court.

Greater freedom of behavior for women was accompanied by growing cynicism (and wild exaggeration) of their actions. Juvenal, writing of a female ritual at the Temple of Chastity, said they went there to "relieve themselves – to urinate on the goddess. They strap a phallus to her statue and take turns straddling it. Early the following morning, a husband on his way to work slips in the resulting puddle. . . ."

The new immorality outraged many Romans who had been raised to believe that female modesty was not only proper but mandatory. The implications of the changed behavior were, however, even more serious. It posed a threat to the stability of traditional family life. The birthrate plummeted. The vast empire had to be administered and policed and the Roman authorities had no alternative but to turn for recruits to the great number of assimilated foreigners whose birthrate showed no similar decline. Emperor Augustus felt called upon to chastise Rome's bachelors:

> What am I to call you? . . . You haven't yet proved your-selves to be men. . . . In the old days, Romans begot chil-dren even on foreign women. But you disdain to make even Roman women the mothers of your children. . . . Not that you live alone, without women. Not one of you . . . sleeps alone. All you wish is freedom for sensuality and excess. . . .

Augustus backed up his reproach with laws which included property disqualifications for childlessness in marriage and for bachelorhood. He tightened regulations for granting divorces. Penalties for lascivious behavior were introduced. (Augustus banished his own daughter, Julia, for her libertine adventures. ". . . the very Forum from which her father had proposed a law against adultery had been chosen by the daughter as the place for her debaucheries. . . .")

Augustus sought to promote old, austere Roman virtues and a revival of enthusiasm for sober, venerable Roman deities. Many had attributed the change in moral standards to the influence of rituals and beliefs associated with Cybele, Astarte, Mithras, Isis and other divinities of foreign origin. Indeed, temples of Isis and other divinities imported from the East were reputed to be hangouts for prostitutes and places where priests and female worshipers engaged in salacious practices. According to some Isis cultists, the goddess herself had served as a sacred prostitute at one time, as an example to mortal women.

But it wasn't only external influences which undermined the efforts of Augustus to combat what he considered moral decline, to restore the sanctity of family life, and to strengthen social cohesion in Rome. His puritanical edicts went against

the Roman grain and proved impossible to enforce. Ironically, one result was to increase libertine behavior among
some women. The punitive measures against loose living did
not apply to prostitutes. This led some women to dress and
make themselves up to look like whores to evade suspicion of
law violation.

Though considered vaguely disreputable, prostitution was
not a despised profession in ancient Rome. Roman whores
were considered merchants of pleasure, sellers of sexual
delights. No one could detect much gallantry, glorification or
romance in Martial's flattering comments to a prostitute past
her prime:

> . . . your hair is manufactured far away and you take out
> your teeth at night . . . and your face doesn't really sleep
> with you. . . . Still you provide me with endless delights.

Even stern Cato, whose mere kill-joy presence could smother
any sort of revelry, publicly counseled, "When a young man's
veins swell with lust, he should go to a brothel rather than
grind some husband's private mill."

Though Rome produced some notably beautiful, talented
and witty courtesans – including Cyrené who was known as
Dodecamechanos ("she of the twelve ways") because she had
mastered a dozen procedures for making sexual pleasure
more intense – none could ever aspire to the heights of respec-
tability and influence attained by their Greek counterparts.
That would have required a glorification of the pleasures of
sex which the Roman context couldn't really accommodate.
Enjoying sex was one thing, exalting such enjoyment was
another – uncouth, gross. On the Roman stage, courtesans
were usually portrayed unsympathetically, often as money-
grubbers.

There were a great number of brothels in Rome. At many
of them the girls and women lingered outside to attract passing men. Other prostitutes were readily identifiable street
walkers, their faces heavily made up, and attired in brightly
colored togas and tunics rather than the discreet long stolas

worn by respectable women. During the Empire, prostitutes were taxed, the tax amounting usually to a daily sum equivalent to the earnings from a single client. By law, brothels were not permitted to open their doors until evening. But many inns were staffed with girls who provided the same service for men who preferred not to wait till sundown and pastry shops often installed working prostitutes to attract customers. No serious effort was made by the authorities to police these violations of ordinances governing whorehouses. Even less official interest was directed at taverns in the countryside, though there was rarely much difference between them and brothels.

Nocturnal street-walking prostitutes were nicknamed "nightmoths." Some who plied their trade at cemeteries were called "grave watchers." They sometimes doubled up as professional mourners during the day to make ends meet.

A favorite place for street-walking whores to take their clients was the sheltered area under the arches –*fornix* in Latin – of aqueducts. The word fornication derives from that practice.

Like those working in large cities today, some prostitutes rented accommodation to which they brought their clients. Many were to be found living and working near the Circus Maximus, where they were particularly in evidence during and after gladiatorial events. They were said to have been kept particularly busy after savage spectacles in the arena had stirred onlookers to a high pitch of excitement.

Brothels were generally divided into small rooms to each of which a prostitute was assigned by the brothel keeper. Affixed to her doorway, or just above it, was a notice of the girl's name and the lowest price she would accept. The money had to be paid in advance. When a girl received a client, she hung a notice on the door of her cell, saying "occupied."

Although a number of Roman writers testified that the brothels were evil smelling, filthy places, visiting one was not considered degrading. In fact, it was thought proper for a Roman youth to receive his adolescent sexual education in such establishments.

The remains of one of the several brothels in Pompeii give an idea of what such places looked like in Roman days. Pompeii was buried under layers of volcanic ash from Vesuvius when the volcano erupted in AD 79 and a record of the city's life and customs was thereby preserved. Still to be seen in those ruins are faded frescoes of erotic scenes – though not as clear and specific as other wall paintings of copulating couples and erotic statuary salvaged from the remains of private Pompeii villas and now part of a special collection at the National Museum in nearby Naples.

An inscription found on the wall of a brothel in the doomed city read HIC HABITAT FELICITAS ("Here Dwells Happiness"). To indicate that it wasn't only the brothel keepers who were satisfied with the service they offered, graffiti on outside walls testified to the experiences of clients: "Lucialla makes it worthwhile" "Arphocras got what he wanted from Drauca for a denarius [a gold coin]."

Though consorting with prostitutes bore no stigma, Ovid, the most eminent writer of erotic literature in the ancient world, counseled a different sort of pursuit for supreme sexual satisfaction. His detailed prescriptions were for the seduction and conquest of desirable married women. ("The crops are more abundant in fields belonging to others. The neighbor's herd has richer udders.") The more difficult the conquest, the more intense the erotic pleasure when it was finally, calculatedly achieved.

To that end, Ovid offered step-by-step advice, the sum total of it reading like a battle plan or a formula for winning at games. Where to seek out a potential mistress: "do your hunting in the arenas where women go to see and be seen" or at dinner parties, the theater or even in the street. How to approach her: if direct contact is difficult or inadvisable, cultivate her maid; her husband's friendship can also be helpful. How to look: "your toga must be neat and free of stains; your tongue must be supple; your teeth unstained. . . . A bad haircut can spoil the look of your hair." On specific action when the time is right:

A practiced lover mixes words with kisses,
But you must take them if they are not given.
Maybe she will object at first and call it outrageous.
But despite her fighting, she hopes to lose.
Only be careful.
Do not kiss too roughly and make her cry.
Remember also that if you stop at kisses,
You do not deserve even those.
To stop at kisses is dull, not virtuous.
Although it is called using force,
Women love to be forced.
They love to be made to give in.
If you take a girl by storm, she adores it.
If she manages to emerge intact,
She may look relieved, but it is only pretense.

Ovid also prescribed methods to be employed to keep a mistress's affections ("be sure she thinks you are spellbound by her beauty"), including advice on sexual method. The final part of his *Art of Love* is devoted to amatory advice to women who, Ovid was convinced, were as anxious to be seduced as their seducers were to bed them down. "Care brings you beauty. Neglect will destroy it.... A narrow face wants divided tresses.... A round face needs a knot above the forehead." "If you are small, sit down or you will appear to be sitting even when you are standing.... A pale girl should clothe herself in purple...." "Make your smile a moderate one, with two neat dimples, and let your lower lip hide its teeth...." "Do not neglect the art of graceful walking. The way you walk can make a stranger fall in love with you."

The Golden Ass by Apuleius offered a different dimension of literary erotica. It was partly an adventure story, constructed around the character of Lucius who was turned into a donkey and then was involved in a variety of escapades. In one of them, for example, he is sexually assaulted by a woman. "She flung one leg over me as I was on my back and attacked me with rapid thrusts of her thighs and passionate wrigglings of her supple hips."

Judging from what has survived of it, attitudes in Petronius's *Satyricon* were even less restrained. They are marked by a hungry indulgence in sexual performance, both hetero- and homosexual. While also an intriguing insight into Roman behavior, it is best remembered for a story it contains which has since been revived and rewritten by many successive writers. It concerns a widow so grieved by the death of her husband that she goes to stay with his remains in his tomb, without eating, till she too succumbs to death. But while there, she becomes enamored of a soldier on duty in the cemetery, guarding the crucified body of a thief. Their presence there together takes its toll and while the soldier and the widow are embracing, the thief's body is stolen. The soldier thereupon announces that he will kill himself for so neglecting his duty. Rather than see her new love join her old love in death, the widow has the soldier raise the body of her beloved husband onto the cross so that no one will notice his negligence, and they continue with their passionate embraces in the tomb.

This story displays a rogue element of romantic love, smothered, however, by the generally ribald setting of the *Satyricon*. It is, in fact, a mockery of old love, savaged by new carnal pleasure. But other hints of sentiment also kept creeping into Roman erotica. The playwright Plautus, whose works are sprinkled with libertines and prostitutes, had a flair for the tender side of sensuality as well:

> *When a lover holds his mistress,*
> *When they press lip to lip,*
> *Tongue to tongue,*
> *Breast to breast,*
> *Their bodies interwoven,*
> *She pours nectar for her lover.*
> *No room there for frowns, scowls or idle chatter.*

The medical-emotional value of erotic literature was detected by the Greek physician Theorus Priscianus who practiced during the late Roman Empire. To cure masculine impotence, he counseled, "Let the patient be surrounded by beautiful girls or boys. Give him books to read which stimulate lust."

The priestesses of Vesta, goddess of the hearth and spirit of the happy home, were virgins and highly privileged religious figures. Those few Vestal virgins who were found to have violated their oaths of sacred chastity were condemned to be buried alive. The diligence with which such a severe sentence was administered depended on prevailing attitudes toward sexual morals – less-than-chaste behavior by Vestal virgins was overlooked during permissive periods.

There was, however, no guarantee that it would be. Divine retribution for the misbehavior of these priestesses could suddenly and unexpectedly be declared the cause of military defeats and other public calamities. After the battle of Cannae, it was discovered that two Vestal virgins had been guilty of fornication prior to that historic confrontation, in which Hannibal's forces trounced the Romans. Their transgression was widely held to be the cause of the defeat. One committed suicide before she could be, like the other, executed.

After military setbacks for Roman legions, laws were sometimes introduced imposing public modesty on women. These, for example, forbade them to wear clothes of bright or mixed colors or extravagent jewelry in public or to engage in "unseemly" behavior. Observance of such statutes, and their enforcement, tended, however, soon to lapse.

Such a hodgepodge of fickle sexual standards and do's and don't's was reflected in the behavior of Rome's rulers. Some of its emperors were reputed to be virtuous and austere. Others were not. Emperor Tiberius, stepson of the stern Augustus, was said by the historian Suetonius to have "taught children . . . to play between his legs while he was in his bath. Those who were still very young . . . he set at fellatio, the pastime best suited to their inclination and age." Tiberius's successor, Caligula, whose bizarre cruelties indicated that he was mentally unhinged (by aphrodisiacs, it has been suggested), "respected neither his own chastity nor that of anyone else. . . . Valerius Catullus, a young man of consular fashion, publicly announced that he had violated the emperor and had worn himself out in commerce with him. . . . There was also incest with his sisters, one of whom he violated when he was still a boy. . . . There was hardly a woman of rank he did not approach. Generally he invited them to dinner with their husbands. . . . He would look them over . . . as if buying slave girls. . . . Then he would leave the room and send for the one who pleased him most . . . Returning later with telltale signs of what had transpired, he would openly praise or criticize the woman, listing her charms or shortcomings." Among Caligula's other eccentricities was visiting Roman brothels at night, bewigged for disguise.

For Messalina, wife of Emperor Claudius, sex was said to be a compulsive driving force. She had actors summoned from the stage to her bed in the course of plays in which they were performing. She sent to the far corners of the empire for officials who had taken her fancy and with whom she wanted to copulate. She would pass nights in Roman brothels pretending to be a common whore and was said once to have challenged a prostitute known for endurance to a contest over which of them could take on the greatest number of men in quick succession, and to have won easily. Messalina's sexual adventures led finally to her doom. Inebriated by sexual license and the failure of Claudius even to reproach her mildly, and presuming he knew nothing, she went so far as to formally marry one of her lovers, though she was still empress. Fed up finally, Claudius had her put to death.

Emperor Domitian was said to have considered copulation a form of physical exercise, "bed wrestling" he called it. He had a harem of concubines and was said to have shaved off their pubic hair with his own hand, a peculiar pleasure for an emperor of mighty Rome. The brief reign of the transvestite emperor, Heliogabalus, was described by one historian as a "four-year debauch."

Some moralists have contended that the spread of sexual permissiveness and the emphasis on erotic pursuits were contributing factors in the decline and fall of the Roman Empire.

Serious historians have repeatedly demonstrated that the real causes lie elsewhere. It can be pointed out that other civilizations, like that of ancient Greece, were permissive virtually from the outset and developed impressively nevertheless before beginning their decline.

It is true that sexual permissiveness signaled the decay of such old Roman virtues as sobriety, propriety and moderation. But that was only a symptom of change, not the cause. Some of Rome's finest moments coincided with some of its most permissive periods. Conventional virtue was on its way back to popular favor when the weight of empire grew too heavy for Rome to carry and when the stage was set for the Vandals and others to relegate the glorious Roman Empire to the history books.

From *The Elegies* of Propertius

How happy is my lot! O night that was not dark for me:
And thou beloved couch blessed be my delight! How
many sweet words we exchanged while the lamp was lit
and how we tangled when the light was gone! She strug-
gled with me with breasts uncovered, sometimes veiling
herself with her tunic to slow me down. With a kiss she
unsealed my sleepy eyes. . . . How often we shifted our
positions and varied our embrace; long my kisses lingered on her lips. . . .

There is a certain Phyllis who lives . . . on the Aventine.
When sober, she does not please me much; when drunk,
she is charm itself. Another is Teia who lives near the
Tarpeian groves. She is fair but when she has had her fill
of wine, one lover is not nearly enough for her. I summoned those two to help me pass the night less morosely
and to renew my amorous adventures. One little bed
there was for the three of us. . . . Do you ask how we
managed ? I lay between the two of them. . . .

From *The Love Epistles*, **by Aristaenetus**

As Hippias t'other day and I
Walked arm in arm, he said
"That pretty creature dost thou spy
Who leans upon her maid?
She's tall and has a comely shape
And treads well too, I swear.
Come on — by this good light we'll scrape
Acquaintance with the fair."
Good God! cried I, she is not game
I'm sure for you or me.
Do nothing rashly — you're to blame.
She's modest, you may see.
But he, who knew all womankind,
Thus answered with a sneer:
"You're quite a novice, friend, I find.
There's nothing modest here.
A virtuous dame this hour, no doubt,
Would choose to walk the streets,
Especially so decked out,
And smile on all she meets.
Her rings, her bracelets, her perfumes,
Her wanton actions prove
The character which she assumes
And that her trade is love.
See now, she fidgets with her vest
To settle it be sure,
And not at all to show her breast,
Not wishing to allure. . . ."
So up he marched and made his bow,
No sooner doffed his hat
But lover-like, he 'gan to vow
And soon grew intimate. . . .
Assent sat smiling in her eyes
Her lilly hand he seized
Nor feigned she very great surprise

81

Nor looked so much displeased. . . .
Hippias was now quite hand in glove
With her and firmly bent
To take her to a bower of love.
His whispered as he went.
"Well say now whose judgment's best.
Was I so very wrong?
You saw, not eagerly I pressed,
Nor did I press her long. . . ."

From *The Satires* of Juvenal

The strange rituals of the good goddess (*Bona Dea*) turn infamous when the strains of the flute stir the loins of her women worshippers. They rush along, moaning and wailing, jerking their heads about, drunk with something or other, randy, man-hungry. Listen to the way they grunt and yelp as their lust intensifies. See the steady stream dripping down their thighs. . . . These are no games, no make-believe. Every movement is dead serious, enough to stir the aged testicles of a doddering Nestor or Priam. The longer they go without, the more excited they get and from all corners comes the shout, "Where are the men!" If their lovers are not available, other studs will do as well. If not enough of those are around, they will settle for slaves. If slaves are also in short supply, what about the water boy ? If even he cannot be found, a donkey will have to do.

From *The Art of Love*, by Ovid

First then believe, all women may be won;
Attempt with confidence, the work is done.
The grasshopper shall first forebear to sing
In summer season, or the birds in spring
Than women can resist your flattering skill.
Ev'n she will yield who swears she never will.
To secret pleasure both the sexes move,
But women most who most dissemble love.
'Twere best for us if they would first declare,
Avow their passion and submit to prayer.
The cow by lowing tells the bull her flame.
The neighing mare invites her stallion to the game.
Man is more temp'rate in his lust than they,
And more than women can his passion sway. . . .
Doubt not from (women) an easy victory;
Scarce of a thousand dames will one deny.
All women are content that men should woo;
She who complains and she who will not do.
Rest then secure, whate'er thy luck may prove,
Not to be hated for declaring love. . . .

From *The Golden Ass*, by Lucius Apuleius

... she kissed me sweetly and tied a garland around my head. . . . She took a cup of wine, softened it with warm water and handed it to me. Before I had drunk it all, she gently took it from me. Sipping it slowly and looking at me as she did so, she drank what was left. We emptied the jug twice or three times that way. Thus stimulated, I removed my clothes and (she) . . . made no long delay either. She undressed and loosed her hair, presenting her lovely body to me in the manner of fair Venus when she goes under the waves of the sea. "Now," she said, "is the hour of battle. Now is the time of war. Let me see what kind of may you are. . . ." Saying those words, she came to me and embraced me sweetly. We passed all the night in dalliance and pleasure and didn't sleep till morning. . . .

By
Sex Obsessed

By Sex Obsessed

It is good for a man not to touch a woman.

— SAINT PAUL

MATTHEW OF AVIGNON, a virtuous man and a friar, was awakened one morning by the noise of a young woman opening his bedroom door. So fearful was he of surrendering to unchaste thoughts that he immediately stripped her and whipped her savagely for placing him in moral jeopardy. Matthew was a man of the Middle Ages and his behavior, perverse and brutal though it now seems, was at the time an object lesson in righteousness.

The Middle Ages, ushered in by the fall of Rome and climaxed by the first stirrings of the Renaissance, were obsessed with sex. But the obsession was nothing like the sexual permissiveness that had been a feature of earlier times. The Roman Empire disintegrated and as the Catholic faith took root in what had been its precincts, it carried with it the conviction, suggested by Saint Paul and propagated by the Church fathers, that sex was depraved and wicked. The disasters which had overtaken and overwhelmed Rome were seen as God's punishment for its erotic sins.

A new emphasis on spiritual values, rather than earthly rewards, convulsed the imagination of the guardians of public morals. The human body was seen to be a trap for the immortal soul, tempting it with carnal pleasures which offered nothing more than eternal damnation. A new concept of folk hero emerged as laudatory tales were told of husbands and wives who had forsaken sins of the flesh and who lived together as brothers and sisters, of men and women who scorned even celibate marriage, of monks who mortified their flesh to overwhelm the temptations of sexual pleasure – Besarion who slept standing up for forty years and Simeon Stylites who retreated to the top of a sixty-foot pillar and stayed there three decades.

Even such precautions did not always suffice. The saintly but unfortunate Helarion was said to see visions of naked women whenever he lay down on his hard, narrow bed. Saint Jerome, who had fled to the desert to save his soul, wrote:

> Parched by the burning sun, how often did I imagine myself amidst the pleasures of Rome. . . . I, who from dread of hell, had consigned myself to a prison in which my only companions were scorpions and wild beasts, fancied myself among bevies of young women. . . . My mind was aflame with desire and lust seared my flesh . . . Helplessly, I lay at the feet of Christ . . . struggling to subdue my rebellious body.

It was a formidable struggle. Praise was heaped on an old priest who, as he lay on his death bed, drove off a woman who had come to bid him a final farewell, shouting, "Begone, woman! You are straw and there's fire in me yet!"

Chastity, agonizing though it might be to sustain, was equated with virtue. Athenasius contended that the creed of sexual abstinence was Christianity's greatest blessing, the *sine qua non* of righteousness. Saint Cyprian measured the comparative merits of martyrdom and virginity as one hundred-to-sixty. Thomas Aquinas considered virgins, and only virgins, capable of aspiring to the stature of angels.

To dispel sexual desire, Saint Magdalena de Pozzi rolled over thorny bushes till she bled. Until forbidden to do so by her confessor, the Blessed Angela de Fulginio placed hot coals against her private parts to burn away the fires of sexual desire.

Such a climate of puritanical fanaticism did not readily accommodate the erotic arts. The nude, so prevalent in

ancient Greek and Roman painting and sculpture, was a suppressed subject. Some cunning craftsmen managed to cir-
cumvent prevailing taboos and carved sensual images on
church friezes, ostensibly to illustrate pious themes – of Adam
and Eve in the age of innocence or the devil toying with
wickedly lustful women in the age of sin.

Vicarious excitement was derived from stories written
about the licentious sexual depravity of Roman women before
they were converted to Christianity and had their souls saved.
For the most part, the hint of erotic representation, where it
appeared, conveyed a harshly moralistic mood, as when it
depicted snakes and other despised creatures gnawing at
women's genitals. The situation would later change dramatically. But in the early Middle Ages, when men were often
harangued to feel shame for sleeping even with their wives,
erotica remained an undercurrent flowing well below the
surface.

Sublimation of the sex urge was an overriding pursuit. The
inevitable consequence was that sex itself, condemned as vile
lust, was transformed into an ever-present focus of the popular imagination, with escape from its damnable ravages
attainable only through unrelenting vigilance.

Measures to control sexual license had been enacted in Greece
and Rome, but they had been devised primarily for social
purposes – to promote family life and prevent disruptive
public excesses. In the Middle Ages, however, guilt became a
central feature of sexual attitudes, one that would persist, to
greater or lesser extent, from then on.

Women were the culprits. They were daughters of Eve, the
original and inexorable desecrators of man's innate virtue.
They lured men to the fires of hell by their mere presence, by
their mere existence. Clement of Alexandria declared, "Every
woman should be ashamed that she is a woman." Another
medieval moralist warned that the female was "the confusion
of man, an insatiable animal . . . an eternal ruin." Theologians
debated whether women had immortal souls, without which
they could not, of course, enter heaven.

Whether they did or not, they were to be avoided. If that was impossible, men should avert their eyes in their presence and avert their thoughts at all times. It didn't always work. The ascetic Saint John Chrysostom moaned, "How often do we, from beholding a woman, suffer a thousand evils . . . entertaining inordinate desire. . . . The beauty of woman is the greatest snare." Tales were told of virtuous men who, after encountering real or imagined would-be temptresses, purged themselves, often through self-flagellation with whips kept within easy reach at home for the purpose. Saint Francis was said to have plunged naked into the snow in winter to subdue his cravings when he was afflicted by thoughts of carnal desire.

For some, even such measures as these were not enough. Tertullian revealed that, while women were "the Devil's gateway," the gates of heaven were open to eunuchs. The philosopher Origen was among those who rid themselves of the danger of damnation through lust by castrating themselves. Surgeons able and willing to perform the necessary operations were said to have suffered no scarcity of patients.

This course of action was not always left to choice. One of the great tragic love stories of medieval times is that of the prominent twelfth-century philosopher and teacher Peter Abelard who, at the age of forty, fell deeply in love with Heloise, the seventeen-year-old niece of a senior clergyman in Paris. When Heloise, who passionately returned his love, bore his child, the outraged uncle and a group of his followers, as Abelard later wrote, "cut off the parts of my body with which I had performed the deed which had distressed them." Such things happened elsewhere as well. Members of a sect known as the Valesians took it upon themselves to castrate others (as well as themselves) to save them from sinful thoughts and the hellfires to which such thoughts would lead.

Despite their firm conviction that carnal satisfaction was evil, the guardians of public morals wrestled in anguish with the conundrum of whether universal chastity was advisable. They were forced to recognize that it was, in fact, an impossible, even irreverent, proposition. Wise and pious they might be, but they had not been empowered to decree the extinction of the human race. As logic gradually penetrated the turgid shroud of anti-sexual superstition, philosophers wriggled uncomfortably in search of theological loopholes to sanction what was inevitable. It was increasingly argued that since man was made in God's image, mankind's admittedly shameful urges couldn't be all bad. Pope Gregory the Great announced that the only thing seriously wicked about copulation was the pleasure derived from it. If that shortcoming could be overcome, he suggested, perhaps sex between husband and wife, necessary for the perpetuation of mankind, might not be sinful.

Going even further, there was growing acceptance of the bawdy revelry which marked pre-Lenten Carnival celebrations in many parts of Europe. Derived from a pagan orgiastic festival, Carnival antics were recognized even by somber moralists as a tolerable, brief fling before the confining moral restraints of the austere days of Lent.

Establishing standards for permissible sexual indulgence was only part of the problem. The attitude and behavior of the clergy, the custodians of the morals of their flocks, often (particularly in the later Middle Ages) conflicted with theologians' preachings on celibacy. In many parts of Europe, priests openly took wives and/or concubines in defiance of their superiors. An archbishop of Canterbury, offended by the practice, felt called upon publicly to order the English clergy to give up their women. A bishop of York considered it necessary specifically to forbid priests from seducing nuns. An abbot of Evesham was described as "a scorner of monastic rule" and, euphemistically, "a friend of women." A bishop of Liège in Belgium was also known for his promiscuity and sired no less than sixty children. In Germany, "priest's child" (*pfaffenkind*) meant bastard. An archbishop of Sens in France expelled monks from a local abbey and established a harem for himself there.

Monks were repeatedly counseled to exhaust themselves with hard work to restrain nocturnal temptations which, they reported, raged through their dreams. In formulating standards of penance for various sins by monks, distinctions were made between different sexual acts they committed – fornication, buggery, bestiality, homosexual acts, nocturnal emissions, and so on.

Practices which were scandalously less than celibate were known to be common in many monasteries and convents. Pope Gregory XII said that many nuns "fornicate with their priests, monks and lay brethren." When a convent in Strasbourg was struck by lightning, a nun and a boy were found suffocated in bed together. It was subsequently discovered that the nuns there had been training male foundlings they raised to become their bed companions. A fourteenth-century chancellor of the University of Paris charged that "cloisters of nuns have become . . . brothels of harlots." Nuns and other women were subject to hallucinations in which they believed their breasts had been fondled by the hand of God and more than one were convinced that they had been made pregnant by Jesus.

Heretical religious movements, some of which flourished in medieval times, promoted their own attitudes toward sexuality. In *The Pursuit of the Millenium*, Professor Norman Cohn describes the Amaurians, thirteenth-century religious anarchists who, it was said, claimed that each of them was God. They were said by the Abbot of Saint Victor near Paris to have "committed rapes and adulteries and other acts which give pleasure to the body. And to the women with whom they sinned, and to the simple people whom they deceived, they promised that sins would not be punished."

Condemnation of sexuality in the Middle Ages clearly had limited impact. Often only meager efforts were made to mask defiance of anti-sex preachings. Except when smitten by lethal epidemics, the population undeniably grew rather than declined. Bastardy was commonplace. Nor were bastards in disgrace, not with such distinguished legendary or historical personalities as William the Conqueror and the Irish warrior Cuchulain numbered in their ranks.

Prostitution was widespread, despite sporadic efforts by

various potentates to root it out when it seemed to be getting out of hand. As early as the sixth century, Theodora, Byzantine empress and reputed herself once to have been a sexually insatiable courtesan, had emptied the brothels of Constantinople in a spurt of moralistic fervor, and had exiled the girls employed in them. Charlemagne placed a ban on prostitution in his European realm. King Philip Augustus of France, in an effort to control prostitution in Paris, went so far as to build a wall around a cemetery there to keep whores from using it as a work place. His grandson, Louis IX, decreed the abolition of prostitution in France in 1254. The ban proved so futile and unenforceable that it was withdrawn two years later.

Prostitution could not be eradicated and some respected theologians even doubted whether it should be. Saint Augustine (who contended that until the fall of man in the Garden of Eden, there had never been erect penises) accepted that the practice served a useful function. "Remove the prostitutes," he said, ". . . and you will contaminate all things with lust. . . . Remove the sewer and filth will be everywhere." Despite itself, the Church felt compelled to condone the existence of brothels and streetwalkers. In some cases, it promoted prostitution. In several places, Church authorities took responsibility for policing brothels, requiring, among other things, that whores did not neglect their prayers. Bishop Boniface reported that some women on religious pilgrimage paid for their travels by selling themselves en route.

Wandering bands which crisscrossed Europe during the early Middle Ages included women who sold themselves to earn their keep in towns through which the wanderers passed. In some towns, there were so many of them regularly proffering their services in the streets that their activities were restricted by the authorities to the hours of darkness. Feudal lords had always had unrestricted sexual access to occupants of their female servants' quarters (in addition to the so-called "right of the first night," priority right to copulate with the brides of their serfs on their wedding nights – while the lowly husbands waited their turn). Town brothels in the Middle

Ages were an urbanized outgrowth of the sexual hospitality of female servants offered by the gentry to distinguished visitors at their feudal estates. As cities expanded and urban populations grew, similar services were required in them. Recruiting women from among itinerant whores, town brothels were designed for the convenience of travelers, local merchants and artisans, and soldiers. The brothels were taxed and licensed. (Licensed prostitutes in Nuremberg are known to have protested to the burgomeister about unlicensed, cut-price competition.)

"Stews" (brothels) were first licensed in London in 1161, during the reign of Henry II. Among regulations governing them was one which prohibited prostitutes from shortchanging their clients: "no woman is to take money to lie with a man but she lie with him all night till the morrow."

Brothels proved to be profitable enterprises. Giovanna I, Queen of Naples and Countess of Provence, founded a lucrative brothel in Avignon within strolling distance of a monastery. Pope Julius II founded a brothel in Rome where at one point the population of 70,000 was said to include 7,000 whores. (The figure is clearly an exaggeration but gives an indication of how numerous the Roman prostitutes were.) The Archbishop of Mainz reportedly maintained prostitutes in ecclesiastical buildings. Dukes of Austria owned brothels in Vienna. Nor were any efforts expended on concealing either the ownership of these houses or the impressive profits derived from them.

Camp followers congregated around garrisons and (as the name implies) accompanied armies on the move. Special sergeants were assigned quartermaster duties for controlling their supply and availability. Small armies of camp followers attached themselves to the Crusades. Embarkation points in southern Europe swarmed with those unable to gain passage to the Holy Land along with the crusaders.

In his *Story of Civilization*, Will Durant quotes an Arab historian as noting that at the Crusader seige of Acre in 1189, "300 pretty Frenchwomen . . . arrived for the solace of the French soldiers . . . for these would not go into battle if they

95

were deprived of women," apparently inducing the Saracen forces to require similar amenities.

Whores were also often employed by town authorities to grace festivals and festivities with their charms. Brothels were sometimes "booked" for the exclusive use of visiting dignitaries and their coteries, as was the case in the cities of Berne and Ulm when Holy Roman Emperor Sigismund visited them, a gesture which moved him to make generous public expressions of imperial gratitude. (Later, hundreds of prostitutes, naked or scantily clad, and crowned with garlands of flowers, would be positioned to lead a reception for one of Sigismund's imperial successors, Charles V, when he visited the thriving merchant city of Antwerp.)

The Crusades had at least a peripheral impact on the sex habits of returning Crusaders. Chastity belts, lockable metal girdles designed to prevent women from copulating in the absence of their husbands, were modified to guard also against extramarital rear-entry copulation after men returned with a taste for what was believed to be popular mideastern sexual diversions. (The more elegant chastity belts were, incidentally, trimmed with red velvet and had artistic designs etched onto them.)

The Crusades were also marked by an increase in homosexuality, attributed by some commentators to mideastern influence, by others to circumstances which brought fighting men together for unfamiliarly long periods of time. Surveying developments, an abbot of Clairvaux in France moaned that "ancient Sodom is springing up from its ashes." Philip the Fair, King of France, asserted that homosexuality was rife among the Knights Templar, a crusading military and religious order which he then proceeded profitably to persecute.

By the late Middle Ages, the heavy hand of the official but futile gospel of chastity had been compelled to relax its grip sufficiently for the erotic arts to bud once more. It was to be a gradual, cautious emergence but undeniable in its reflection of changing public attitudes toward the propriety of sexual display.

The nude, scrupulously neglected for centuries, again emerged into public view. At first, deference to residual taboos confined artists to tame subjects. Naked figures, most often set in the Garden of Eden or at the Last Judgment, were depicted in postures of shame and humiliation, to mollify the lingering puritanical ethic. With the passage of time, however, increasingly bold, unapologetic erotica emerged, gracing the friezes and altarpieces of magnificent Romanesque and then Gothic churches which, with their soaring spires, similarly mirrored the growing emancipation of the human spirit. The somberness of the earlier cautious dabbling with previously forbidden themes gave way to explicit realism which was to blossom in the erotic works of such masters as Van Eyck and Cranach. Their graceful nudes were dignified as well as sensual, having discarded the inhibiting vestiges of shame and guilt.

An element of mischievousness had also appeared. Comically grotesque gargoyles in the form of phalluses and the lower regions of squatting female figures often served as water spouts on churches and castles. Magnificently detailed church friezes sometimes showed monks dallying with nuns. Such pranks were also played in medieval literary erotica when it too finally pushed past confining prohibitions. The *Exeter Book*, one of the earliest specimens of English literature, included some of the first post-Classical dirty jokes. Among its riddles, it asks, what is:

> a peculiar thing which hangs by a man's thigh under his clothes. It is pierced in front, stiff and hard. . . . When the man lifts his garment, he plans to pay a visit with . . . this hanging tool to the familiar hole which it . . . has often filled before.

The answer – a key – must have caused much merriment in the monasteries where such riddles were devised.

The more substantial and more widely disseminated erotica of the period also displayed an earthiness which had thoroughly overturned obsessions with sexlessness. In Chaucer's *Canterbury Tales*, the Wife of Bath is casually promiscuous and her behavior does not seem sinful. The Goliards produced an irreverent litany of praise for the carefree life. The Goliards were an amorphous collection of wandering students, minstrels and defrocked priests who declined to accept repressive moral dogma. They refused to believe – or even to pretend to believe – that this world is a vale of tears, a testing laboratory, a mere prelude to eternal existence in heaven for those who emerged with their souls untarnished and their bodies undefiled. The joy of sex was a refrain which ran through Goliard ballads, expressing sentiments like these:

> *To drink and wench and play at dice*
> *Seem no great, mighty sins . . .*

> *When I think of a maiden's breasts,*
> *What thrill my wayward hand would feel*
> *To fondle those incomparable hills.*

The thirteenth-century French *Romance of the Rose* was equally forthright in its sensual imagery:

> *Women call them catch-alls, harnesses, torches, things,*
> *And even pricks,*
> *As if they were thorns.*
> *But after they have been properly introduced,*
> *They do not really find them so painful.*

Once the doctrine of chastity was proved untenable, the pursuit of sexual restraint was channeled along different paths. If women were not instruments of the Devil, new roles had to be formulated for them, consistent with altered standards of moral behavior. Connubial bliss, though even that had been deemed wickedly deceptive by some, became the approved state for adults. Promiscuity and erotic display were increasingly evident but they remained intolerably sinful.

To fashion a transformed image for the once-despised female, a romantic milieu gradually developed in which the ideal woman became an object of respect, even of veneration. An age of chivalry produced a body of romantic literature which told of gallant knights who dedicated themselves to rescuing damsels in distress, who galloped off in search of hazardous good deeds to be performed on behalf of their ladyloves. These knights were described as chaste and virtuous. As often as not, it was said, they worshiped their women from afar, some even swooning with love at the mere sight of them. Some performed absurd rituals, like carrying flasks of water in which their ladies had washed, to refresh their spirits and ardor while on their errands of chivalry. They spawned the legends which fostered the age of "courtly love" and which were to nourish romantic concepts of love right to the present day.

However, the actual habits of the knights, whose adventures troubadours and storytellers subsequently immortalized in their ballads and tales, were somewhat different from what they were made to seem. They had, in fact, perpetrated what the guardians of public morals would have deemed barbaric excesses. Their exploits were later laundered, probably unwittingly, to meet a need for heroes who, despite their manliness, could coexist with newly elevated women without ravishing them as warriors had previously done (and often still did).

Among the most celebrated of the heroes of the Age of Chivalry were the gallant knights of King Arthur's Round Table. But Gildas, a British monk who chronicled the period, described them as "boastful, murderous, addicted to vice. . . . They are generally engaged in plunder and rapine. . . . They are fornicators and adulterers." Another historian suggests that "the first thought of every knight on finding a lady unprotected was to do her violence." It was not unusual for them to take their women by force, often seizing them on the road as they traversed the countryside on what would later be described as glorious errands of chivalry. Germanic knights were said to be so ravaged by their carnal vices that many "died of old age before they were thirty." William of Malmesbury described the Norman nobility, which was subsequently renowned for its chivalry, as immersed in "gluttony and lechery."

Like many of the legendary lawmen of the American West, the wandering knight was often simply a glorified brigand or mercenary. He was an experienced horse-soldier prepared to employ his skills to get what he wanted. He was not part of the ethic of sexlessness which the songs of the troubadours emphasized to create a climate of untouchability for desirable women in the age of courtly love. He emerged through the twilight of Dark Age promiscuity in Europe in which, incidentally, promiscuous propensities were not exclusively confined to knights in not-so-shining armor.

Robert Briffault, who examined their exploits, wrote that if a knight "performed a service on behalf of a lady, the latter was . . . bound in honor to reward him with her favors, a pledge which she had in general little reluctance in fulfilling." It was not unusual for the lady to make the first overtures in such situations. Nor was the approach on her part considered improper. In even expurgated legend, the gallant Gawain complements his paramour for offering herself to another brave knight and a beautiful lady pacifies her cuckolded husband and lord by assuring him that her knightly lover is a warrior of great reputation.

At jousts, ladies were known to heighten the excitement of the contests through their own devices. Arriving primly attired from neck to toe and from wrist to wrist, with their heads adorned with fashionable examples of the medieval milliner's art, lady spectators often shed items of clothes, wafting them toward competing knights whom they favored to cheer them on. Despite the formality of the occasion, the knights in the lists were suitably aroused by ladies who, by combat time, were left suggestively bare-armed and bare-headed.

Ladies were known to serve jousting knights whom they favored in more intimate ways as well. After the contests, they often bathed and massaged them, put them to bed, and were not averse then to slipping in alongside them.

Even during the heyday of romantic chivalry, when it was popularly believed that knights of yore had been virginal and breathtakingly valiant, it was not unusual for young gallants, seeking to ape their ways, to indulge in carnal pleasures which the legends implied were unthinkably unchivalrous. It was an age of indecision and contradiction about the character of women.

Harking back to earlier warnings about sexual deceptions and perils, Andreas Capellanus could write in his twelfth-century *Art of Courtly Love*, "no woman, no matter how famous or revered, will reject the embraces of any man, even the most wicked and lowly, if she thinks he is skillful at the work of Venus; but no man . . . can satisfy the desires of any woman . . ."

Such warnings had little bearing on sexual behavior. The riddle for an hypothetical man of the late Middle Ages who might have been baffled by such contradictions was: how could women be fair game for any aroused males (and therefore inferior) when celebrated troubadours kept singing ceaselessly about ladies fair who were to be adored untouched (and therefore superior). In fact, those ballads, like sentimental romantic stories and songs of later days, served an important function. They erected a framework of respectable living myth behind which exuberant sexual life of the times could shelter. Chivalry was a hoax to begin with, adorning woman with a spiritual prestige which masked her subservient status. It conveniently produced a catalogue of genteel formalities and niceties to satisfy ethical codes which were based on prevailing moral instruction but which had little to do with reality.

101

From *Carmina Burana*
(Thirteenth-century poems of the wandering Goliards, discovered, in
Latin, in a Bavarian monastery in the nineteenth century.)

. . . give me rouge to dab on my cheeks,
So men will not spurn my charms.
Look at me, sir. Am I not pretty?
Make love, make love.
Love will exalt you,
And earn you admiration . . .

Ah, my pretty girl, come to me.
I wait for you, for you alone.
Come to me, my pretty girl.

Lovely red lips,
Come and end my pining,
Come and end my pining,
Lovely red lips . . .

When a boy and a girl
Are together, alone,
They are linked by joy.
Their desire builds
And shyness flies away.
Indescribable joy oozes
Through their arms, their legs, their lips.

From *The Wife of Bath's Prologue, The Canterbury Tales*,
by Chaucer (1340-1400)

Did God at any time insist upon virginity? Everyone knows that when St. Paul spoke of it, he said there was no law governing it. A woman may be advised to be a virgin, but that is only advice. It has been left to us to decide. If God had insisted upon virginity, he would have forbidden marriage. If that had happened, and no one was ever born, where would we find virginity?. . . Some prefer to remain unsullied in body and soul. I will not claim such perfection. . . . For what purpose were our organs of procreation made? And what were we made for? Not for nothing. . . . I do not condemn virginity. Let virgins be bread of the best flour and call the rest of us inferior loaves. But, as St. Mark told us, it was with such loaves that our Lord Jesus fed the multitude. . . .

Regenesis

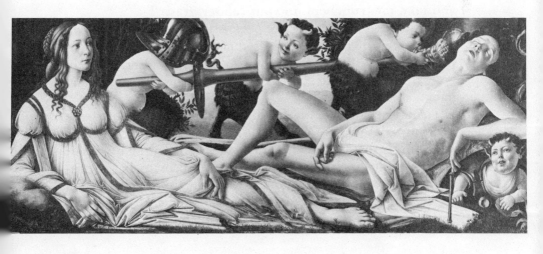

Regenesis

A woman not possessed of . . . rare grace can no more abstain from a man than from eating, drinking, sleeping or other natural functions. Likewise a man cannot abstain from a woman.

– MARTIN LUTHER

IN THE EXTROVERT, headstrong era which we call the Renaissance, the medieval cloak of virtue and the veil of professed innocence were brushed irreverently aside. It was the age in which Fallopius, seeking a preventive for venereal disease, invented the contraceptive sheath. It was when well-educated youngsters, attuned to the rediscovery of Classical lore and brushing up their Cicero and Catullus, knew the Latin equivalents of "prick" and "cunt." It was a period in which poet Pietro Aretino, a sometime adviser to the Pope, could compose such lines as, "Place your leg, dearest, on my shoulder, and take my truncheon in your tender grasp."

Guidelines for what was not permissible could not be drawn for an age when everything seemed possible. Criteria for judging standards of erotic behavior could not be cramped in an era where other aspects of the human spirit were emancipated.

To impose limits on the erotic imagination would have been futile at a time when, for example, Copernicus was proving audaciously that the Earth was not the center of the universe; when Vesalius was dissecting corpses and proving in the process that the heart had more important things to do than shelter an immortal soul; when Leonardo da Vinci was toying with plans for a machine in which people might actually fly ;

106

when John Wycliffe was proclaiming that man needed no intercession by priests to commune with God; and when doubt spread about whether God really objected to sexual indulgence.

Things were fundamentally different. Luther could call the German town of Erfurt "nothing better than a brothel and a beerhouse." Henry VIII ordered the closure of London's brothels, following which one of his bishops asserted, "There is now more whoredome in London." In France, Brantome noted, "Among great folk . . . rules and scruples about virginity are made little of. I know many girls who did not take their virginity as far as the marriage bed."

The Renaissance was an age of exploration and discovery, experiment and change, sincerity and sham, honesty and deceit, improbable truths and plausible hokum. Medieval emphasis on spiritual values had given way to a focus on human thoughts, feelings and actions. As in our own age of technology, breathtaking logic led from one Renaissance innovation to another.

Not by chance did the discovery of the Americas coincide with the exploration by Giorgione, Titian and other master artists of the exotic dimensions of female voluptuousness. Not by accident did the era which begot the study of anatomy also begot the sketches of Giulio Romano which examined the various postures of copulation. The invention of the printing press, one of the major milestones of the Renaissance, facilitated the dissemination of an extensive body of erotic literature, including the writings of Boccaccio, whose works bubbled with tales of sex-hungry men and women finding carnal fulfillment; of Brantome, a chronicler of the erotic games people played; and of Rabelais, the first to write about truly gargantuan sexual appetites. In liberating the human spirit from the already crumbling confines of medieval ideological narrowness, the Renaissance unfettered a long-bridled aspect of the erotic urge – sex became fashionable.

Torn free from even a semblance of the restrictive orderliness of medieval feudal links, an emerging, questing middle class recognized few limits to human endeavor. This sense of daring proved contagious. Kings and princes bent with the wind and most often were content to rule over the new, vibrant order.

Renaissance vitality touched off a sprawling range of ideas and movements which probed relentlessly into what previously had been unknown, inscrutable or unmentionable. Public attitudes toward erotic display were transformed. Chastity, so long extolled, came to be seen as having far less merit than sexual prowess. Virility and allure became cardinal virtues. Fashions in attire began to emphasize male genitals and female bosoms.

The well-dressed Renaissance dandy wore brightly colored tights to which were laced, or otherwise attached, a distinctive bag-like codpiece which housed his penis. These codpieces were often padded for effect and accentuated with colorful bows and decorative fastenings.

Women's blouses and the bodices of their gowns crept lower and lower and were often drawn in so tightly that the breasts ascended. In some places, breasts were exposed and nipples rouged as the height of daring fashion. Though the French poet Ronsard could boast of indiscriminating tastes in women ("Is she plump or is she lean, my pleasure is the same"), it was an era when breast fetishism (the bigger, the more exciting) was rampant among men. A poem of the period begins:

> *Bosom, thou art complete perfection;*
> *Bosom, of silky white complexion.*

Cosmetics were extensively used. Some women still resorted to a lead mixture to whiten their faces, but more sophisticated cosmetics were also developed, based on, among other things, plant substances and egg white. In France a concoction made largely of bear's fat was much in favor among fashionable women. A contemporary English observer commented that his countrywomen "colour their faces with certain oyles, liquors, unguents and waters ... whereby they think their beauty is greatly decored." The Italian poet Ariosto mocked:

108

How many little knives and scissors for the nails and little cakes of soap and slices of lemon for the hands. They need an hour to wash them and another hour to annoint and rub them until they are perfect. And how many powders and how much work are needed to clean the teeth. I could not count the number of boxes, phials, little bottles and other trifles that they use. You could fit out a ship from stem to stern in less time.

Perfumes of various kinds, including musk, ambergris and civet, were widely and excessively employed for sprinkling over clothes as well as for dabbing all over the body. Scents were used by men as well as women, partly because bathing had largely gone out of fashion and because of the stench of the streets in the rapidly mushrooming cities.

The erotic arts had new stimulus. There wasn't really all that much ground to cover between enchanting, emotive late medieval madonnas and the coy nudes of the early Renaissance. The love poems of Petrarch, one of the early literary giants of the Renaissance, contained elements of spirituality which deferred to earlier restraint as well as sensual imagery for the new frontier of tolerance. In fact, explicit sexual themes in art not only were tolerated as they hadn't been since the Roman Empire, but became chic as well. The sensual lines and beauty of the unclothed human form were rediscovered with passion in painting and sculpture.

Giorgione's nude *Venus* covers her pubic hair with her hand but it's a casual posture, devoid of shame or modesty. She is a beautiful, desirable, accessible woman. The nude in Titian's *Sacred and Profane Love* appears to have risen satisfied from a love bed. Michelangelo poured his homosexual passion for the male form into the strong, rippling lines of his statue of *David*. Correggio's masterful full-frontal *Antiope* is as provocative as the most teasing of modern pinups. Raphael's *La Fornarina*, the first erotic portrait, is a lush representation of the artist's mistress with her bosom bared.

The nude was an obsession with the Renaissance painters. "It seemed," wrote Kenneth Clark in his study of the subject, "that there was no concept, however sublime, that could not be expressed by the naked body, and no object of use, however trivial, that would not be better for having been given a human shape."

Artists were themselves erotically inspired by the sensual imagery their skills evoked, by the circumstances through which their creations took shape, and by the privileged positions conferred on them by admiration for their work. Sculptor and master metalsmith Benvenuto Cellini casually commented of a young woman, "I keep her mainly for the sake of my art. I must have a model. But being a man as well as an artist, I have used her for my pleasure too." The artist Giovanni Antonio Bazzi earned the name *Il Sodoma*, by which he is still known to art historians, because of the way he flaunted his homosexual appetites. It was during this period that artists developed the reputation they retain for being promiscuous and morally lax.

Erotic orientation extended at the time with similar thoroughness to the theater. There was much kissing and suggestive touching on stage and plots more often than not centered on sexual pursuits. If Don Juan was a rogue for deflowering respectable females, he was at least a resourceful rogue, with an admirable appreciation of sensual pleasure. His treachery was thus a perverse honesty and the Spanish audiences which were the first to see him on the stage were as much impressed by his amorous successes as they were humored by his ultimate damnation.

Young and old alike delighted in public circuses and spectacles which featured stallions mounting mares. City-center brothels proudly hung out floral displays to broadcast the presence within of newly signed-on virgins. The call on their services was so great that they could claim virginity – and the floral displays could be flaunted – for longer than was strictly possible. Barmaids and chambermaids were generally accustomed to performing sexual services for transient guests. Everyone knew those services were also readily available in certain sections of all major cities, on "Gropecunt Lane" in

London, for example, or on "Slut's Hole Street" (*Rue Trousse Puteyne*) in Paris.

The prostitutes' quarter in London was south of the Thames in an area mostly under the jurisdiction of the archbishop of Canterbury and the bishop of Winchester. In Paris, it was on the left bank of the Seine, in what would later become the Latin Quarter. A guide for visitors to Venice listed the names and whereabouts of the city's more desirable prostitutes and their charges. (Young and pretty prostitutes had lower per-client tax rates than their less attractive sisters because their turnover was greater.) Valencia was among several cities which employed doctors to make sure registered whores were not infected with venereal disease.

The Church's official attitude toward erotica and sexual indulgence was ambiguous, where not totally undefined. Some of the Renaissance popes were generous patrons of the arts who assembled fabulous collections which included some of the most exquisite erotic images ever put on canvas. (One Vatican room is still kept locked and barred to visitors though it has been suggested that the erotic masterpieces it houses were long ago seriously damaged by the ravages of time and neglect and are now virtually indecipherable.)

Pope Pius II fathered two bastard sons. Pope Alexander VI granted his daughter, Lucrezia Borgia, a divorce partly on the grounds that he himself was father of her child. Though the excuse was a politically inspired fabrication, it demonstrates what was then considered credible.

In Germany, Church leaders condemned drunken clergy who staggered from tavern to tavern in search of carnal satisfaction. Citizens of Lausanne protested about clergymen who appropriated the wives of citizens and refused to return them – not only was this highly insulting to the cuckolded burghers of the city but deprived the public brothel of earnings they had previously derived from the adulterous clergymen. A Spanish monk was accused of trying to seduce nuns by explaining that they were obliged to indulge in sexual intercourse with him because they and he were spouses of Christ. Failing with that ploy, he composed prayers laced with erotic imagery which he hoped would inflame their carnal passions.

Nor was the Church alone in its moral confusion. It was as much a characteristic of those times as it was to be of later periods. The genius, scandal-monger and hypocrite Pietro Aretino was the living personification of the more outlandish and brilliant eccentricities of the period. A satirist of international standing, an author of theological treatises, Aretino's most enduring achievement – repeatedly translated and imitated – were erotic poems, vividly descriptive verse:

> . . . *less chatter (he has a woman say);*
> *Fuck me now,*
> *Pierce my heart and soul with a mighty plow*
> *Of that mighty prick which is life and all to me;*
> *And while you do it, see*
> *That the twin attendants of my greatest pleasure,*
> *Those balls of yours, are included for good measure.*

Aretino was one of the earliest outspoken defenders of erotic arts. He condemned "that miserable propriety which forbids our eyes to see what pleases us most. What harm is there in seeing a man mount a woman? Should animals enjoy more freedom than we do?" This ringing proclamation lost some of its impact when the same Aretino denounced as intolerably obscene the erotic works of an artist he considered a personal rival.

But it was really not remarkable that distinguished personalities should produce erotic imagery. The talents of a true "Renaissance man" were varied and impressive. Philosopher Niccolo Machiavelli, most famous for his advice to rulers on the deceptions necessary for maintaining political power, was author also of *Mandrake*, the first modern bedroom farce, in which a man seduces a virtuous but desirable woman with the unwitting assistance of her husband. Rabelais, who had one of his characters counsel building city walls out of women's vulvas because they are more resistant than bricks to wear and tear, had been a physician as well as a monk. Brantome, who vividly portrayed the mood of sexuality of the period, was a soldier and a courtier as well as an author.

112

The Renaissance was very much a masculine era, marked b[
great emphasis on virility, manliness and masculine achieve[
ment. But, in contrast to medieval times when women gaine[
prominence either as threats to the virtue of men or as th[
untouchable, adored creations of troubadours, females were
humanized in the Renaissance, known finally to be individual[
capable of feelings, thoughts and accomplishments, though
those remembered for their achievements are comparatively
few in number.

Caterina Sforza ruled the cities of Forli and Imola in Italy
for eleven turbulent years – no modest feat. Sophia, wife of
Ivan III, was influential in ending Tartar sway in Russia.
Christine de Pisan was a much-acclaimed French poet whose
verse emphasized the dignity of women. Margaret Beaufort
was a co-founder of English colleges.

But the Renaissance women who made the most notable
mark on their times were courtesans – women of beauty, wit,
charm, intelligence and discretion, women who fashioned
themselves after the celebrated hetaerai of ancient Greece,
women who entertained and amused the prominent men of
the period. Such a woman was Imperia Cognata, who had a
succession of the richest men in Rome as her lovers. Such a
woman was Jeanne le Coq, the principal mistress of Francis I
of France, who considered beautiful women to be works of art
and always kept a selection of them nearby. When Francis
traveled around France, he moved with his court – sometimes
with as many as 15,000 people in all: officials, servants,
soldiers, and a specially chosen stable of courtesans under the
care of a royal madam.

The word "courtesan" originally meant merely lady at
court. It was during the Renaissance that it came to mean a
superior class of prostitute, well-educated, witty, lively women
who often kept their own "courts," salons where men of distinction would congregate for intelligent conversation and
distraction.

The courtesan did not take the place of the wife. For men
who were their clients, marriages to other women were almost
always arranged by relatives. Families with wealth, rank and

social status could not leave such matters to chance or whim – the ownership of property and land was involved. But young men of the upper classes not only usually found their sexual pleasures away from their carefully selected wives – aside from siring heirs, they were expected to do so.

As in some other periods, women were considered sexually insatiable creatures who required continuous child-rearing, rigorously self-imposed modesty or regular copulation to avoid going mad. Though middle- and lower-class married women were expected to behave modestly, widows were said to be openly sex-starved. An Elizabethan proverb counseled, "He that wooeth a widow must go stiff before." Another saying of the period contended that though "fifteen hens will satisfy one cock, fifteen men are not enough for one woman."

In fashionable society, seduction by men was a legitimate, even a compulsive objective. It confirmed the virility of seducers in an age which placed high value on individual distinction and in which it was widely held that no husband could possibly meet the sexual demands of his randy wife. In literature and on the stage, a husband could easily be made to appear ridiculous defending what he took to be his wife's honor. But her seducer was never anything but heroic, no matter what buffoonery he had to perpetrate to bed her down.

In high society, a woman without a lover felt obliged, for the sake of her reputation, to invent one. In plays and stories, the husband was invariably outperformed sexually by both the lover and the wife. It gave rise to a lasting image of a man who was both the inconsiderate husband of one woman and the accomplished lover of another.

Royal courts of the period tended to be places of dalliance, promiscuity and general sexual playfulness. Francis I, who occasionally wandered in disguise through Paris to amorous trysts, enjoyed hearing his courtiers recite stories of their sexual adventures and had many of his own at court. (It was reported once that when visiting the chambers of one of his court mistresses, he spied a courtier in her room trying to hide

114

in the fireplace, behind some leafy boughs placed there for decoration. Uttering no word of reproach or recognition, the king urinated through the boughs into the fireplace and left, having enjoyed himself thoroughly.)

Elizabeth, the virgin Queen of England, was said to be profoundly shaken by the randy courtiers and ladies around her who indulged in pleasures which the queen, dedicated to her calling, felt she could not politically afford. Inevitably, it was rumored that she had a succession of secret lovers, if only to retain her mental balance for the sake of England.

Innovations in domestic architecture during the period had an important effect on courtship habits. Bedrooms began to be walled-off areas, introducing an element of privacy which strongly influenced sexual habits. The development allowed for greater emphasis on preliminary wooing and sex play. As Lewis Mumford pointed out in his *Culture of the Cities*, "[It] gave rise to a new code of sexual manners, embroidering the preliminaries of sexual intercourse, and tending to lengthen the period of amatory youth for both sexes." Women began receiving guests in their bedchambers as casually as they do in their living rooms today. It made for increased opportunities for sexual involvement. Bedroom innovations had their impact even in houses of the poor where private bedrooms remained rare. Featherbeds to lie upon increasingly replaced straw pallets on beds and pillows replaced logs as headrests. Sexual intimacies in bed became less rough, hasty and uncomfortable.

There were, of course, voices raised in protest against the erotic revolution. Sexual guilt and shame, nurtured during the Middle Ages, had planted deep roots which would continually sprout – in different places at different times. Even during the comparatively tolerant Renaissance period, learned doctors served notice that immoderate sexual activity could lead to blindness, gout and other maladies. Young men were warned that serpents lay waiting within the bodies of virgins to inflict nasty bites on their penises. A Paris prelate at the turn of the sixteenth century chastised local booksellers for peddling "vile, sensual books." An occasional fire-breathing, hell-raising clergyman – like Savonarola – fiercely condemned unvirtuous behavior, sometimes directly challenging the authority of his more lenient Church superiors.

Through his fiery oratory, with which he insisted upon a rebirth of spiritual values and a rejection of worldly pleasures, Girolamo Savonarola, a Dominican friar, became effective ruler of Florence from 1494 to 1498. Defying Pope Alexander VI, who futilely instructed him to cease preaching, Savonarola mounted a vigorous campaign of moral renewal. The crowd-stirring high points of his campaign were huge bonfires in which sinful items were set ablaze, including the writings of Boccaccio, women's ornaments, scents and wigs, and paintings of beautiful women. Those who engaged in public erotic displays or were indiscreet in their private transgressions risked disgrace and imprisonment. But Florentines soon wearied of Savonarola's unrelenting puritanism and after the exasperated pope excommunicated the turbulent priest, he was taken prisoner by the city authorities and tortured. He was said to have confessed to heresy and was quietly hanged.

Other outbursts of reaction against permissiveness took less dramatic form. Towns in Scotland appointed officials to track down "fornicators and fornicatrixes" and shave their heads or have them pilloried or banished. In England, many thousands of convictions of sexual crimes (including fornication, adultery, buggery, incest, bestiality and bigamy) in rural regions during Elizabethan days indicated that the ordinance under Henry VII a century earlier to "eschew the Stynkynge and Orrible Synne of Lechery" had not yet expired, at least as far as the lower orders were concerned. The English clergyman and scholar Robert Burton asked, "Of woman's unnatural, insatiable lust, what county, what village doth not complain?" The Dutch philosopher Erasmus advised, "When undressing, when arising, be mindful of modesty and take care not to expose to others anything that morality and nature require to be concealed." The Devil himself, so active in medieval times, intervened once more.

Lust and promiscuity, often falsely attributed to others by sex-crazed abstinents, were seen as the Devil's domain in regions where puritanical authorities exercised power. Even those falsely charged with succumbing to fornication through Satan's wiles were exposed to cruel tests of their innocence. When the water test was applied, women accused of being witches were immersed in water – if they floated, they were witches; if they drowned, they were innocent.

Ironically, at a time when the flowering of the arts and the scientific imagination signaled an end to superstition, witchcraft threatened to become a specter haunting Europe (surfacing later in the American colonies). The Devil himself lurked behind every erotic suggestion. *Malleus Maleficarum* ("Witches Hammer"), a Church-sponsored study of ways to detect and prosecute witches, declared, "All witchcraft comes from carnal lust, which in women is insatiable." Men were warned against succubuses (female demons) which materialized in their bedrooms at night to fornicate with them and thus lead them to perdition. Incubuses (lecherous male demons) were said to be given to nocturnal visits to women's beds.

The most rigorous steadfastness and piety had to be practiced to ward off damnation, especially as trafficking with Satan's minions was now a civil crime as well as a sin. The Devil himself might choose to ravish a woman. Those accused of succumbing to him were brought before inquisitorial courts where, after torture, some of them revealed that he came equipped with a huge, scaly, frosty penis which, despite its dimensions and character, did not hurt. Nor did it leave traces of penetration and even those women who could claim physical evidence of virginity were not immune to accusations of having fornicated with the Prince of Darkness. Frantic imaginations conjured up orgiastic witches' sabbaths in which damnable sexual trafficking with demons was the high point and for which accused witches were condemned to death.

Women who aroused erotic feelings through their looks, dress or demeanor were often suspected of being witches.

How else could they have had the effect they did on men?
Confession after torture rarely saved their lives; their crimes
were too grave. Death through burning was a common punishment, though repentance before execution could save
their souls from the fires of hell.

From *Lives of Fair and Gallant Ladies*, **by Abbé de Brantome (Pierre de Bourdeille)**

. . . in which provinces and regions of our Christendom and Europe (be there) most cuckolds and harlots? Men declare that in Italy the ladies are exceedingly hot, and for that cause very whorish, as saith M. de Beze in a Latin epigram to the effect that, where the sun is hot and doth shine with most power, there doth it the most heat women . . . Spain is in the like case, though it lies more to the westward; yet doth the sun there warm fair ladies as well as ever it can in the East. Flemish, Swiss, German, English and Scotch women, albeit they . . . inhabit cold regions, share no less in this same natural heat ; and indeed I have known them as hot as dames of any other land.

The Greeks have good reason to be so. . . . And in sooth they do possess many attractive points and merits . . . seeing in times of old they were the delight of all the world and have taught many a secret to the ladies of Italy and Spain from ancient times even to the present day. . . . And verily was not Venus, the queen and empress of all harlots, a Greek? As for my fair countrywomen of France, in old days they were notoriously very coarse and unrefined, contenting themselves with doing of it in a coarse, rude fashion. But beginning some fifty years ago, they have borrowed so much and learned from other nations so many gentle ways, pretty tricks, charms and attractions, fine clothes, wanton looks or else themselves have so well studied to fashion themselves therein, that we are bound to say that they do now surpass all other women in every way. So I have heard even men of foreign nations admit, they are better worth a man's having than any others, not to mention that naughty words in French are more naughty, better sounding and more rousing than in any other tongue.

From *Malleus Maleficarum* ("Witches Hammer")
(Summary of witchcraft compiled by Jakob Sprenger and Heinrich
Institoris and first published in 1487.)

All other wickedness is nothing compared to the wickedness
of a woman. . . . She is an enemy of friendship, an unavoid-
able punishment, a necessary evil, a natural temptation, a
desirable calamity, . . . an evil of nature, painted with pretty
colors. . . . Terence says that women are intellectually to be
compared with children. . . . She is more carnal than man, as
is obvious from her many carnal abominations. It should be
recalled that the first woman was defectively formed because
she was made from a bent rib, the breast rib. . . . Through this
defect, she is an imperfect creature, always deceiving. . . .
Truly we may agree with Cato of Utica who says that if the
world could be rid of women, we would not be without
God. . . . A woman is beautiful to look upon, contaminating to
the touch and deadly to keep.

From *Le Cent Nouvelles* (The Hundred Stories)
Fifteenth century

The knight saw that the miller's wife was very pretty and buxom and said to her, "Forgive me, young woman, but I must tell you that you appear to be in serious trouble. . . . I can clearly see that your frontal is in danger of sagging precariously. In fact, it can't be long before it collapses altogether. . . ."

"Oh, woe," the woman wailed. "What about my husband ? He won't want me any longer !"

"It is not as bad as all that," the knight said. "There are effective cures. . . . I can tell you how to remedy your affliction and protect your frontal. . . . The way to do it is to have your frontal perforated as often as possible."

"Where can I find someone who does such a thing?"

"I, myself, am willing to administer the remedy."

They proceeded, the knight and the miller's wife, to the mill where they began the cure immediately. . . . In short order, the knight, employing a tool he had with him, perforated the miller's wife's frontal three or four times. She was much relieved and pleased. When it was done . . . an appointment was made for the next treatment.

From *The Lives of Married Women*, **by Pietro Aretino**
(1492-1556)

He exposed his fiery-headed, volcanic, wart-embellished stump and, whipping it about a bit, announced, "It is completely at your service, my lady." She let the thing rest on the palm of her hand and cooed, "Nice little duck, sweet birdy, nice pigeon. Into your aviary now. Come into your castle. This fortress is yours!" Resting up against the wall, she lifted a leg, slid it in under her belly and had it standing up. I felt like an ape licking its lips in anticipation. Had I not resorted to a metal pestle lying nearby, which smelled as if it had been used for crushing cinammon, I might not have been able to survive watching the pleasure of others. The mighty lance did its job. But the woman, though tired, had not yet had enough. She sat down on the side of the bed and, grabbing the generous purveyor, stroked it, caressed, sucked it and kissed it so much that it rose again. But she was not much taken by its master's looks so she turned her back on him and had him that way. . . . When the second encounter was over, she called out to me, "There is still some left for you!"

From *To His Mistress Going to Bed*, by John Donne
(1572-1631)

. . . *your gown going off, such beauteous state reveals,*
As when flowery mead th' hills shadow steals.
Off with that wiry coronet and show
The hairy diadem which on you doth grow:
Now off with those shoes, and then safely tread
In this love's hallowed temple, this soft bed.
In such white robes, heaven's angels used to be
Received by men; thou angel bring'st with thee
A heaven like Mahomet's paradise; and though
Ill spirits walk in white, we easily know,
By this these angels from an evil sprite,
Those set our hairs, but these our flesh upright.
License my roving hands, and let them go,
Before, behind, between, above, below.
O my America! my new-found-land,
My kingdom, safeliest when with one man manned,
My mine of precious stones, my empery,
How blest am I in this discovering thee,
To enter in these bonds, is to be free:
Then there where my hand is set, my seal shall be.
Full nakedness! All joys are due to thee,
As souls unbodied, bodies unclothed must be,
To taste whole joys . . .

Lust
and Reason

Lust and Reason

With arms, legs, lips close clinging to embrace,
She clips me to her breast, and sucks me to her face.
Her nimble tongue, Love's lesser lightning, played
Within my mouth, and to my thoughts conveyed
Swift orders that I should prepare to throw
The all-dissolving thunderbolt below.

— THE EARL OF ROCHESTER, *The Imperfect Enjoyment*

NOTHING HAS EVER DONE more to provoke an explosion of erotic indulgence than puritanical repression. Such was the case in England in the seventeenth century when the Puritans – the same breed of men as some of America's Pilgrim Fathers – ruled England for eleven years and then were forced to make way for a licentious royal Restoration.

An age of rigid sexual repression was transformed practically overnight into a period in which the Earl of Rochester, one of the covey of rakes who strutted and womanized at the Restoration court of Charles II, could boast that Britain had "famous grown for breeding the best cunts in Christendom."

The king's father, Charles I, had been dethroned and decapitated by puritans. Though Charles II was a dedicated lecher, politics as well as pleasure was at play in this permissive outburst. Anything unpuritanical had, by definition, much to commend it in post-puritanical, anti-puritanical Britain. Sexual squeamishness would have been suspect in palace circles – and in little favor in most other parts of the land. Licentiousness was virtually tantamount to proof of loyalty to the new regime.

Charles himself was perhaps the only British king who ever allowed himself to be sensually fondled and stroked by his lady companions in public. He had, and flaunted, a string of mistresses and was inclined to visit London's brothels as well. The English adaptation of the contraceptive sheath ("English overcoats" they were called in France at the time) was said to have been devised by a Dr. Condom (hence the name), reportedly a physician at the court of Charles II.

Few restraints were imposed on erotic allusions conjured up by Restoration playwrights and poets. William Wycherley's play, *The Country Wife*, for example, is the story of a lothario who noises it about that he has been castrated, in order to allay the suspicions of the sharp-eyed husbands of desirable women and thus get them to lower their guard against him. In one of its bawdy scenes, the protagonist has the wife of a trusting local dignitary feel for herself, in the presence of her deceived, laughing husband, that he is, in fact, still in full possession of his private parts. King Charles was so delighted with Wycherley's work that he appointed him tutor to one of his illegitimate sons, the Earl of Richmond.

The sexual license of the Restoration coincided with the spread of permissiveness in many parts of the western world. It was, in part, stimulated by the implications of the spread of economic individualism, by the leeway for purely personal behavioral decisions such a development permitted, and by the need to escape from the pressures such decisions could imply. Earlier permissive attitudes – a product of the Renaissance awakening – had flowered at different times in different places. Morally austere reactions to them, and to other practices which offended moralists, were perhaps inevitable. The teachings of John Calvin had been disseminated in the sixteenth century from Calvin's Geneva bailiwick where men and women who so much as danced together were liable to be imprisoned and fornication was punishable by drowning.

In Spain, where the Inquisition had bitten deeply, fear of sinful erotic suggestion ruled feminine clothes fashions – bodices were stiffened with wire and whalebone in such a way as to eliminate any suggestion of seductive curves. Lawmakers in the English colony of Massachusetts felt the need to keep close watch on public behavior because, they declared, it was "a common practice in divers places for young men irregularly and disorderly . . . to insinuate [themselves] into the affections of young maidens, by coming to them in places and seasons unknown to their parents."

But American colonial life was largely without a stern, stoical tradition. The practice of "bundling," in which a young man and woman, usually fully dressed and usually in the presence of others (albeit in a darkened room), engaged in bed in usually low-keyed love play, had successfully been transmitted from Britain, Holland and Scandinavia by early settlers. In some parts of the colonies, it was called "tarrying." It existed in a setting where homes were small, usually consisting of only one room, fuel was in short supply both for lighting and heating, and where long work hours limited the opportunities for couples to court, particularly in winter. "Bundling" also sometimes referred to the tradition of hospitality in remote regions where a passing stranger was permitted to share a bed for the night in an isolated farmhouse. Sometimes it was the bed of the young woman of the house which he shared, from which practice the bawdy "traveling salesman" stories evolved.

The American colonial fathers condemned "bundling," as they condemned extramarital indulgence generally. But even they did not flatly object to sexual pleasure. If such pleasure was part of marital bliss, they chose to make little fuss about it and indulged contentedly themselves. The celebrated puritan clergyman Cotton Mather, famous for his austere moral code and his warnings about the temptations of the devil, was married three times and fathered fifteen children.

But in Britain, according to historian G.M. Trevelyan, puritans, who considered even the mildest flirtation sinful and wicked, made "constant and obtrusive demands for professions of religious zeal upon the common occasions of life. [They] made men 'eat religion with their bread' till the taste of it sickened them." The overthrow of these puritans and the return of the monarchy was widely greeted with relief, even by many who had little to gain from it, as was the relaxation of repressive official standards of sexual morality.

New standards were fashioned which, in many places, required at least tacit observance by those in the public eye. Max von Boehn, in his history of *Modes and Manners*, points out, "Even if he did not feel drawn to any lady but his wife, a ruler was in honor bound to satisfy etiquette by taking a mistress, if only a nominal one." Thus Frederick I of Prussia (1688-1713) made the gesture by taking up reluctantly with a countess at his court. Augustus the Strong, a German prince who became King of Poland (1697-1733), found it politically expedient to take a Polish mistress, though he already had many German ones. (He acknowledged fathering more than 350 bastards.)

But the indulgences of many other monarchs and aristo-crats had little to do with expediency. The Margrave of Baden-Durlach, a German princeling, kept a personal harem of more than one hundred ordinary whores. In France, a succession of kings, while usually more fussy in their choice of sexual partners, were no less wanton. Louis XIV had a succession of mistresses without damaging his image of piety or adversely affecting the reputations of the women involved (quite the contrary!). The mistresses of his successor, Louis XV, among them three sisters taken in succession according to age, included the famous Madame de Pompadour who was cultivated by foreign diplomats in Paris because of the influence she had with the king. (When he had wearied of her carnal attractions but not of her friendship, she was permitted to choose a harem for the king.)

The great French erotic painters of the period, notably Boucher and Fragonard, were court painters. Much of their work mirrored a fun-loving attitude toward sex. Voluptuous nudes, copulating deities from Classical mythology, pastoral scenes of innocent dalliance – what Shakespeare had called "country matters" – these themes recurred repeatedly. Louis XV commissioned Boucher to paint a series devoted to rustic erotica, including scenes of a girl fondling a boy's penis and of copulation in the fields. It was said that the purpose was to help the king's timid grandson, later to be Louis XVI, to learn the facts of life. Whatever he learned from those paintings, Louis XVI did not inherit the erotic inclinations of his predecessors and was to be known throughout Europe as a prude.

Libertine shenanigans at royal courts in various parts of Europe, the subject of titillating gossip everywhere, percolated down through society, somewhat tempered en route by residual concepts of decorum and propriety, by social restraints (ignored by revelers at court), and by the growing atmosphere of grotesque formality that, as we shall see, was gradually encroaching upon normal social intercourse.

Elaborate masked balls in Paris, the pleasure gardens of London and the sprouting beer gardens of Germany were arenas in which commoners might ape the ways of court life – gathering to eat, drink, make merry, flirt, establish liaisons and, where circumstances permitted, as at the Vauxhall Gardens in London, to make love. As the growth of trade and the money economy inflated the class of well-to-do commoners, the fashionable among them joined the aristocracy in flocking to various watering places and resorts – like Spa in Belgium and Bath in England – to partake of pleasures previously reserved for their social betters and to display themselves (much as their descendants would later converge on St. Tropez, Aspen and Kitzbuehel). They inaugurated the daily evening parade of men and women, in their finery, up and down the main streets of those resorts – an occasion for individuals to study "the field," size up desirable individuals of the opposite sex and perhaps even make overtures to be pressed home at a more convenient place at a later time. The practice still survives in the evening *passeggiata* in Italian towns, the *paseo* in Spanish towns and similar displays elsewhere in southern Europe.

The abrupt change in the English moral climate during the Restoration displayed peculiar overtones which were particularly apparent at the royal court, the stage on which attention was most keenly focused. A perverse pattern was established which would subsequently crop up again from time to time.

Desirable women flocked to, and were warmly welcomed at, court. They sought the material rewards of the good connections that could be established there as well as the sensual contact with dashing courtiers. The Earl of Rochester and his cronies could take advantage of the opportunities this offered.

But, as often as not, these men frequented brothels instead, where the available females were neither as fetching as those at court, nor as clean. In one of his poems, Rochester pleads with a bed companion:

> *Fair nasty nymph, be clean and kind,*
> *And all my joys restore*
> *By using paper still behind*
> *And spunges for before.*

The courtiers chose one such brothel as their particular hang-out and the usual venue for their orgies, though more agreeable settings, and the delectable ladies of the royal court, were at the disposal of such well-placed dandies.

Theirs was a deliberate quest for sensual squalor. A kind of sexual anarchy developed for these rakes, as if lifting the puritan restraints had not been nearly enough – or far too much. Rochester and other courtiers deliberately sought to outrage others, becoming exhibitionists, rowdies and trouble-makers, continually tempting fate. In one incident, two of them (Lord Buckhurst and Sir Charles Sedley) barely escaped lynching, after obscenely berating a crowd of Londoners, mockingly exposing their private parts and urinating on those they abused from the balcony of an inn. Rochester deliberately trod even more dangerous terrain by ridiculing the lengths to which he claimed Nell Gwynn, a royal mistress who said, "I am the king's protestant whore," was required to go to arouse the king sexually:

> *. . . the pain it costs to poor laborious Nelly,*
> *Whilst she employs hands, fingers, mouth and thighs,*
> *Ere she can raise the member she enjoys.*

There was, however, a far more significant development in sexual patterns during this period. Nell Gwynn, the king's favorite, was an actress. Madame du Barry, the last and most influential of the many mistresses of Louis XV of France, had been a milliner. The woman Peter the Great of Russia took first as his mistress and then as his czarina was of peasant origin and had been a housemaid. The woman who, later in the period, as Lady Hamilton, became mistress of Lord Nelson, Britain's greatest naval hero, had been a lady's maid and a waitress.

Napoleon was to say that any of his soldiers, no matter how humble, could aspire to greatness, that each of them metaphorically "carried a marshal's baton in his knapsack." During this period, any beautiful, seductive woman, no matter how humble, metaphorically carried a crown, or at least a tiara, tucked in with her cosmetics. Class barriers in sexual relations had begun to crumble at the edges. Social ascendancy through sexual achievement became, for daring women, a career open to looks and talent. And despite a flurry of novels, like *Manon Lascaut*, about the inevitable misery and wretchedness that awaited fallen women, leeway was found for far more tolerant attitudes toward female sexual permissiveness.

Recognition, as it dawned, that women might not necessarily be timid, inferior and subservient had far-reaching consequences. It extended beyond the bedroom and beyond those who observed the influence low-born mistresses of the high-and-mighty could wield. (Cardinal Mazarin, chief minister of France, complained that Spanish men had an unfair advantage over Frenchmen because Spanish women knew their place; "they only make love and do not meddle.")

As setting up a home in a cave had, in prehistoric times, established the pattern for female subvervience to males, the opening of bedroom doors by adventurous, ambitious females in the seventeenth and eighteenth centuries signaled far more than momentary diversions – it signaled the dawn of what would become the women's liberation movement.

Defying residual but potent social restraints on female

erotic expression in the arts, Aphra Behn, the first English women to earn her living through her writings (and, incidentally, a sometime espionage agent in Holland for Charles II), could hint at the descriptive freedom her successors would claim in the twentieth century by explaining in one of her works the rewards a man may derive from marriage:

> Those snow-white breasts, which before you durst scarce touch with your little finger, you may now, without asking leave, grasp by whole handfuls. . . . Now you may practice . . . delicious things to please your appetites and do as many Hocus Pocus tricks more. . . .

The demure, helpless, inhibited female was still very much in evidence and would be for a long time to come (even now!). But a new creature frolicked across the stage: the woman who, though not a whore, assumed audacious, shameless poses in sexual encounters, the kind of poses previously reserved primarily for prostitutes.

Not only was the courtesan's art of out-and-out seduction no longer denied to other females but, in proper society in Paris, Vienna, London and other sophisticated centers, such boldness was considered normal in an attractive woman who had a true claim to the feminine graces. It became increasingly permissible for a female to flaunt her looks and transmit specific sexual signals. She wielded erotic power, bestowing sensual rewards or withholding them according to her desires, whims or schemes. Lewis Mumford, in his *Condition of Man*, pointed out that "a lover was a trophy which one wore as conspicuously as possible," though sexual liaisons were casually made and dissolved.

Fans fluttered flirtatiously at the theater, at balls and in drawing rooms, focusing attention on alluring smiles, seductive glances and powdered, partly exposed bosoms. Beauty spots and patches, tiny bits of gummed black silk or paper, were widely applied. Shaped like stars, hearts, animal figures, crescents, circles and much else, they were worn at the corner of the mouth or eye, above the upper lip, in the middle of the forehead, on exposed parts of the bosom and on other parts of the body which would be uncovered in more advanced sexual encounters.

Women spent hours applying thick layers of rouge and other cosmetics to beautify themselves. Leopold Mozart, father of the famous composer, complained that females were so over-painted that "an honest German cannot tell a naturally beautiful woman when he sees her." The most elaborate hairdos since the Roman Empire were concocted to accentuate feminine attractiveness and allure. Fashions were sufficiently liberated to induce the town council of Leipzig, though females were not particularly notorious there, to prohibit "bodices cut so low as to leave neck and bosom scandalously, impudently and offensively bare." The French began installing bidets for douching purposes. Casanova, the most famous womanizer of the period, announced, "There is no need for whores in this wonderful age. There are as many accommodating decent women as any man could want."

A goodly number of "decent women" became both obliging and emancipated from the restraints of conventional modesty. No less a woman than Catherine the Great of Russia could take and discard a series of lovers without sullying her reputation as a strong and wise ruler. Ninon de L'Enclos, a celebrated Parisian courtesan, summarily summoned and dismissed her prominent lovers as the fancy moved her. (She was the center of a breathtaking tragedy in which her grown-up son, not knowing his origins, fell passionately in love with her and then, learning the truth, killed himself.) A reported incident in which two abbesses in Venice fought a dagger duel over the affections of a handsome abbot, was considered neither scandalous nor in bad taste. The "Enlightenment," so called because of the clouds of obscurities brushed away by the thinkers of the period, was dawning.

It was an age of reason when sexual blinkers were considered old-fashioned, silly, irrelevant and, worst of all, irrational. Some of the most eminent Enlightenment figures testified as much. In France, Denis Diderot, compiler of the first modern encyclopedia, contended that copious copulation was an important ingredient in the good life. He was also author of a novellette in which women's vaginas acquire the power of speech and recount their erotic experiences. Voltaire, the most eminent architect of modern rationalism, chose to deflate the image of spectacular past incidents through a farce he wrote about Joan of Arc in which protaganists turn to making love at moments when they were supposed instead to be making history. In his *Essay on Women*, irreverent English writer and member of parliament John Wilkes was as blunt as he could be. "Life can little else supply," he intoned, "but a few good fucks and then we die."

Despite this climate of erotic license, peculiarly rigid standards of etiquette developed in proper society. Well-bred individuals knew the prescribed ways of dressing, walking, talking, gesturing, sitting, eating. Parisian patterns came to be considered a model for proper behavior – as they would again in some subsequent periods. Books on etiquette in France and those claiming to be based on French practice appeared and circulated in the best circles. Men were advised in them that it was bad form to sip at wine glasses rather than drinking heartily, or to spit into fires the way ruffians did, or to break wind, even in the presence of social inferiors.

There were epidemics of exaggerated hat tippings, flourishes of the hand, snuff-sniffing and similar gestures meant to signify gentility. People were advised to overcome their primitive aversion to the use of the fork, a silly-looking utensil that had recently become popular among the up-to-date French, and to master its use at table to show they were not barbarians. The language of courtship had to be changed. An English book of etiquette, published in 1632, had admonished :

> . . . he that can deliver his mind in amorous words, doth seem to keep the keyes of (a maiden's) Maidenhead . . . while the other poor Lover that cannot express his mind in a complement may pine away with sorrow unregarded.

Such advice to the lovelorn grew, however, increasingly obsolete. Declarations of love, which had previously been suitable and which might have still been acceptable to country hicks and other unsophisticates, were considered downright gauche and gushy among the genteel.

Women were instructed to observe rigid codes of bizarre polite behavior. For many, practically all social intercourse was turned into elaborate ritual. Casanova told of how he met a woman in a carriage with whom he flirted and copulated there and then, only to be snubbed by her when next their paths crossed because, as she haughtily explained, "a frolic does not constitute an introduction."

An etymologist, mathematician, occasional spy, inveterate humbug and man of letters, Giovanni Giacomo Casanova is one of the towering personalities of the literature of eroticism. He devoted the bulk of his voluminous memoirs to his sexual conquests, claiming to have possessed hundreds of women, many of whom he identified by name. The women were of all ranks and shapes and his assignations with them occurred either by design or on the spur of the moment in any convenient venue – in hallways, back streets, boats, not to mention bedrooms.

Casanova's appetites were undeniably extravagant. But he claimed that they were colored by an emotion which, under the liberating impact of the Enlightenment, was to become increasingly considered divorced from sexual involvement. He insisted he *loved* the women he seduced. He loved them "madly" and "passionately." He invariably loved them briefly, however, which casts doubt about the depth of his affections, such doubt being consistent with the standards of an age in which romantic feelings were derided as mumbo-jumbo, mawkish and unseemly. Jonathan Swift dismissed love as a "ridiculous passion" which existed only in "play-books and romances." A French courtier, Compte de Buffon, contended, "Flesh is the only good thing which love has to offer." It caused problems, however, because despite rational pretensions, romantic love between men and women did exist.

The rakish Earl of Rochester touchingly revealed that while he had no sexual problems when engaged on pure and simple carnal pursuits, he was unable to have an erection while lying

with a woman he loved – and cursed his penis for the humiliation:

> *Thou treacherous, base deserter of my flame,*
> *False to my passion, fatal to my fame.*
> *Through what mistaken magic dost though prove*
> *So true to lewdness, so untrue to love? . . .*
> *May'st thou ne're piss, who didst refuse to spend,*
> *When all my joys on false thee depend.*
> *And may ten thousand abler pricks agree*
> *To do the wronged Corinna right for thee.*

A directness of approach to erotic behavior was also mirrored in the diaries and other writings of the period. They
varied in form, content and style and ranged from dry nota-
tions to elaborate prose. But they shared an absence of eva-
sion, subterfuge or embarrassment. The English civil servant
Samuel Pepys, whose diaries provide an insight into the
Restoration milieu, could, in his entries, alternate day-to-day
trivia, matters of personal importance and reference to erotic
adventures – all noted down in revealing, droning mono-
tone :

> . . . from there walked toward Westminster and being in
> an idle and wanton humour, walked through Fleet Ally,
> and there stood a most pretty wench at one of the doors,
> so I took a turn or two. . . . And so to home, where I
> found my wife not well, and she tells me she thinks she is
> with child, but I neither believe nor desire it. . . .

Pepys makes a note in his diary of having read *L'Ecole des
Filles* ("School for Girls") a "lewd book," but only for "informa-
tion sake." This anonymous French novel, first published in
1655, took the form of a discourse between a young woman
and an experienced one about what the latter knows of and
the former expects from sexual pleasure.

The period was soon to see the first flowering of serious,
earthy novels – including *Fanny Hill* and *Tom Jones* – in which
sympathetic men and women indulge in erotic adventures as
part of their development into mature, likeable characters.

Like Pepys a few decades earlier, the Scottish writer James Boswell, best known for his account of the life of the scholar and wit Samuel Johnson, punctuated his diaries with references to sexual temptation and fulfillment. He noted, for example:

> I am surrounded with numbers of free-hearted ladies of all kinds – from the splendid madam at 50 guineas a night down to the civil nymph with white-thread stockings who tramps along the Strand and will resign her engaging person to your honour for a pint of wine and a shilling.

Despite amateur competition, prostitutes were a pervasive feature of all major cities during the Age of Reason. London was reputed at the time to be the most lucrative center for them and it was possible to buy directories of prostitutes there, describing their particular attributes and skills. Young women who pursued the profession converged on the British capital from all parts of northern Europe. But other places managed well enough despite this drain. In Venice, prostitutes peddling their wares were authorized to parade bare-breasted along certain streets. In Berlin, a primitive form of social security for whores was established, with prostitutes making monthly contributions to assure a certain amount of pay-back after they were compelled by age to retire. French and German girls were recruited to supplement the Russian whores who staffed the brothels of St. Petersburg. As a harbinger of things to come, the prostitutes of Paris (they could be banished to Louisiana when it was a French colony for disorderly behavior) were well enough organized toward the close of the eighteenth century to demonstrate against rough handling by the police and the authorities.

Sexual liberation took on a grotesque dimension with the writings of the Marquis de Sade. Others before him had inflicted painful and ugly sexual punishment on both men and women. But none had managed to immortalize such behavior in a series of well-written, obsessive books – among the best known of which are *Justine* and *Philosophy in the Boudoir*. Nor had anyone before managed to bestow a name on such behavior: "sadism" being the desire and ability to derive pleasure from inflicting pain on others. De Sade seemed to be answering the question asked by the English writer John Bulwer: "To what prodigious extremeties doth the abused phantasie of man sometimes drive him?"

The philosophy behind de Sade's behavior has been interpreted as an extension of the concept of liberty to everything which is humanly possible, with an emphasis on the violation of society's most jealously guarded conventions, particularly those related to sexual propriety and criminal activity – "the complete freedom." Others have chosen to interpret de Sade's behavior merely as that of a psychopath who proved his mental unbalance by his cruel sexual abuse of prostitutes in a series of recurring incidents which led to his being confined in prisons and a sanitarium for a total of twenty-seven years. During one stay in prison, he wrote one of his more famous works of sexual perversion, *120 Days of Sodom*, on a single roll or paper, some forty feet long.

Real and professed indifference to and contempt for romantic emotional attachments aroused a reaction toward the end of the eighteenth century. A romantic movement, with the emphasis on profound love rather than passionate sex, gathered momentum and, in places, became pervasively fashionable. To resort to sighs or tears at the slightest emotional provocation became chic. Depth of feeling became admirable. Goethe's enormously popular *Sorrows of Werther*, in which a young man kills himself because of an unhappy love affair, was published in 1774. It touched off an epidemic of suicides in Germany among young people who found their romantic emotions too intense to bear.

There was also, in some places, a widening reaction against what was considered the immorality of erotic freedom. In what would develop during the Victorian era into a wave of puritanism, the sober middle classes increasingly condemned spendthrift, shiftless, unseemly, immoral behavior among the nobility and at royal courts. Some rulers began clamping down as well. Maria Theresa, Archduchess of Austria and effective ruler of the Holy Roman Empire for almost half a century, organized chastity commissions which were empowered to enforce modest behavior in public. Among other things, she ordered that skirt hems, which had been rising, be lowered to respectable lengths and that bodices be raised, but once, when she tried to lecture her chief minister on his notorious loose living, he replied, "Madam, I have come to discuss your affairs, not mine."

From *The Perfect Enjoyment*, by George Villiers, Duke of Buckingham

O heaven of love, thou moment of delight!
Wronged by my words; my fancy does thee right!
Methinks I lie melting in her charms
And fast locked up within her legs and arms;
Bent are our minds, and all our thoughts on fire,
Just labouring in the pangs of fierce desire,
At once like misers wallowing in their store,
In full possession, yet desiring more.
Thus with repeated pleasures while we waste
Our happy hours, that like short minutes passed,
To such a sum of bliss our joys amount
The number now becomes too great to count.
Silent as night are all sincerest joys,
Like waters deepest running with least noise.
But now at last, for want of further force,
From deeds, alas, we fall into discourse;
A fall which each of us in vain bemoans,
A greater fall than that of kings from thrones.
The tide of pleasure flowing now no more,
We lie like fish left gasping on the shore.

From the *Memoirs* of Casanova

At last this Venus stood before me in a state of nature, covering her most secret parts with one hand and hiding one breast
with the other, and appearing sadly ashamed of what she was
unable to hide. Her confusion, this conflict between vanishing
modesty and onrushing passion, delighted me. . . . She grew
gradually bolder. We admired each other and then slipped
into bed. Nature made its demands known and we happily
sought to satisfy it. Carefully, I made a woman of Hedvig.
When it was done, she kissed me and assured me the pain she
had felt could not compare with the pleasure. Then came
Helen's turn. . . . She was jealous of Hedvig and used both
hands to hold herself open to me. Though she went through
much pain before initiation into the mysteries of love, her
sighs were those of happiness. . . . Her great charm and agility
hastened the sacrifice and when I withdrew it was obvious that
I needed to rest.

From *Fanny Hill, Memoirs of a Woman of Pleasure*,
by John Cleland

. . . my lips, which I threw in his way, so as that he could not escape kissing them, fixed, fired, and embolden'd him: by this time, the young fellow, overheated with the present objects, and too high mettled to be longer curb'd in by that modesty and awe which had hitherto restrain'd him, ventur'd, under the stronger impulse and instructive promptership of nature alone, to slip his hands, trembling with eager impetuous desires, under my petticoats. Oh then! the fiery touch of his fingers determines me, and my fears melting away before the glowing intolerable heat, my thighs disclose of themselves, and yield all liberty to his hand: and now, a favorable movement giving my petticoats a toss, the avenue lay too far, too open to be miss'd. . . . I lay palpitating, till the ferment of my senses subsiding by degrees, and the hour striking at which I was obliged to dispatch my young man, I tenderly advised him of the necessity there was for parting, at which I felt as much displeasure as he could do, who seemed eagerly disposed to keep the field, and to enter on a fresh action. But the danger was too great: and after some hearty kisses of leave, and recommendations of secrecy and discretion, I forced myself to send him away, not without assurances of seeing him again, to the same purpose, as soon as possible. . . .

English Folk Song

On yonder hill there stands a creature:
Who she is I do not know.
I'll go court her for her beauty,
She must answer yes or no.
  O no, John! No, John! No, John! No!

On her bosom are bunches of posies,
On her breast where flowers grow;
If I should chance to touch that posy,
She must answer yes or no.
  O no, John! No, John! No, John! No!

Madam I am come for to court you,
If your favour I can gain;
If you will but entertain me,
Perhaps then I might come again.
  O no, John! No, John! No, John! No!

My husband was a Spanish captain,
Went to sea a month ago;
The very last time we kissed and parted,
Bid me always answer no.
  O no, John! No, John! No, John! No!

Madam in your face is beauty,
In your bosom flowers grow;
In your bedroom there is pleasure,
Shall I view it, yes or no?
  O no, John! No, John! No, John! No!

Madam shall I tie your garter,
Tie it a little above your knee;
If my hand should slip a little farther,
Would you think it amiss of me?
  O no, John! No, John! No, John! No!

144

My love and I went to bed together,
There we lay till cocks did crow;
Unclose your arms my dearest jewel,
Unclose your arms and let me go.
  O no, John! No, John! No, John! No!

Turbulent Undercurrents

Turbulent Undercurrents

*When you feel any inclination to go abroad in search of forbidden
pleasures . . . sit down with your sisters and sing*
"Home, Sweet Home."

— ADVICE TO AMERICAN YOUTH FROM
REVEREND HARVEY NEWCOMB

*The man who avoids women and the woman who seeks out
men are abnormal.*

— RICHARD KRAFFT-EBING

*Stooping over the prostrate form, the brawny brute drew out a
monstrous prick . . . [and] drove his trenchant weapon to the hilt in
her gaping quim.*

— FROM A STORY IN THE LONDON MAGAZINE *The Cremorne*

THE VICTORIAN ERA, which straddled most of the nineteenth
century, was a maze of confusion and contradiction. The
period was so weighed down by exaggerated prudishness that
the very word *Victorian* came to mean prim and straitlaced.
But it was also an age scoured by turbulent undercurrents of
erotic activity and suggestion.

Never before had there been so great an outpouring of
literary erotica – from titillating pornographic fantasies to
scholarly bibliographies. In London, the Kama Shastra Society of distinguished scholars translated and published the
erotic writings of the East. In Paris, male university students
(females were not permitted to attend lectures at the Sor-

bonne until the 1880s) commonly cohabited with working girls, who often supported them. The aesthetic imagination probed new visions of sensuality on canvas. With the development of photography, pornographic photos made their debut.

The streets of major cities of the Old World were patrolled by armies of prostitutes. In America, whores (later to be sanitized and glamorized in western movies) were among the pioneers who settled the new towns of the Far West. The brothels and bars where they congregated were often the first community centers of those towns. In respectable Berlin, the Prussian spy-master Wilhelm Stieber ran his notorious "Green House" where high-ranking officials and other dignitaries were offered dazzling sexual opportunities (and were thus set up for possible blackmail). In London, men too repressed or discreet to visit any of the profusion of brothels there could instead attend publicly advertised "anatomy lectures" to ogle naked women. A best-selling French book presumed to advise husbands and wives to treat each other as lovers and mistresses. ("If he tries to undress you, let him.")

Free love became intellectually respectable during the Victorian era and even a battle cry for utopian and libertarian movements. "Yes, I am a free lover!" trumpeted Victoria Woodhull, one of the more outspoken of nineteenth-century American feminists. "I have an inalienable, constitutional and natural right to love whom I may, to love as long or as short a period as I can, to change that love every day I please!" The great French actress Sarah Bernhardt proclaimed, "I have been one of the great lovers of my era."

While philosopher Pierre Proudhon ("Property is theft") contended that housekeeping and prostitution were the only truly suitable roles for women, most of the newly-emerging socialist thinkers (especially those who called the family a capitalist institution in which wives were enslaved) believed in equal rights – and, by implication, equal sexual rights – for men and women, though some feared that such rights would lead to work competition with men and to lower pay for all. Feminists, utopians and other radicals were influential in promoting the use of contraceptive devices and methods to free women from the threat of unwanted pregnancy without limiting their sexual opportunities.

The emancipated woman made her debut in the nineteenth century, sometimes broadcasting her emancipation through petty acts of defiance, like smoking in public or wearing men's clothes. Others, like Victoria Woodhull, sought more basic expressions of freedom. French novelist Amandine Aurore Lucie Dupin, who took the name George Sand to formalize her personal liberation, sought elusive sexual satisfaction through conspicuous bohemian behavior and occasional promiscuity. As everyone was permitted to know, she included the poet Alfred de Musset and the pianist Frederic Chopin among her many lovers.

This was, however, the same period when prevailing public attitudes amounted to a moral conspiracy, the central doctrine of which was that sexual pleasure was shameful and squalid. This conspiracy was less effective in France than in most other places because restrictions on sexual indulgence there were often made to seem absurd and unnatural. But even in France, romantic idealization of the untouchable female, camouflaging a low regard for women generally, tended to insulate females of the middle classes (and wherever middle-class virtues were influential) from erotic thought or practice.

In the United States, Anthony Comstock, founder of the militant New York Society for the Suppression of Vice, successfully agitated for legislation strictly banning the dispatch of "obscene" material through the post and claimed to have been directly responsible for the destruction of 160 tons of pornography. United States Surgeon-General William Hammond lent official sanction to the anti-sex movement by contending that only one time in ten does a woman experience any pleasure in sex (presumably because woman was, by nature, virtuous and pious). In England, Dr. William Acton, a wise and accomplished physician and medical scientist, declared, "The majority of women, happily for them, are not much troubled by sexual feelings of any kind." It was fashionable to believe that a woman who indulged in the task of supplying her husband with children did so sacrificially and that, when copulating, she merely lay still and let her husband get the distasteful, dreary act over with as soon as possible. Said Acton: "The best mothers, wives and managers of households know little or nothing of sexual indulgence. Love of home, children and domestic duties are the only passions they feel. As a general rule, a modest woman seldom desires any sexual gratification for herself. She submits to her husband, but only to please him and, but for the desire of maternity, would far rather be relieved from his attentions."

Sexual urges were considered degrading. The well-meaning English statesman William Gladstone made nocturnal rounds of prostitutes' haunts in London to induce them back to the paths of righteousness and then went home to lash himself with a whip because of the lascivious thoughts those visits aroused in him.

For a man to desire a woman physically was considered depraved. Hardly a prude, French philosopher Jean Jacques Rousseau had written of a woman, "I loved her too much to wish to possess her." That sort of romantic renunciation of sexual love worked itself into Victorian moral ideology, with perverse consequences. It meant, in effect, that a man could "possess" only someone for whom he had no respect, much less love. That was why the brothels kept so busy.

Ironically, the French Revolution, though an historical libertarian upheaval, had had sexually repressive overtones. Unlike the American Revolution thirteen years earlier, which had no immediate impact on the balance of social classes, the Revolution in France signaled the overthrow by the middle classes of monarchical and aristocratic rule. It would have been reasonable to expect such an upheaval to be accompanied by permissive sexual attitudes.

To some extent it was. But, at the time, moral standards prevailing under the rule of kings and aristocrats were for the most part seen to have been corrupt and unvirtuous, libertine rather than libertarian. Those standards had to be changed. A sturdy thread of sexual puritanism thus was embroidered into the garb of revolution, particularly in attitudes toward women. The old, elaborate façade of courtesies that had been erected for dealing daintily with women, while seducing them, was deemed to have been reactionary. Women had to be knocked off their high horses, but not, however, to be treated as equals. In view of the facade of privilege previously built around them by etiquette (even Louis XIV, the Sun King, was known to have tipped his hat to a dairymaid), females were now obliged to stand well back and let men get on with the job of fashioning a new civilization. (The *Code Napoleon* was soon to formalize, in terms of modern law, the subservient position of women in society.)

Nevertheless, the fiery revolutionary principles and lofty sentiments which were let loose upon the world spawned the earliest modern expressions of feminism. Olympe de Gouges promulgated a *Declaration of the Rights of Women* in Paris in 1791 and Englishwoman Mary Wollstonecraft (mother, incidentally, of the authoress who was to create *Frankenstein*) published her *Vindication of the Rights of Women* in London a year later.

The momentum of revolutionary verve momentarily punctured some of the restraints on sexual indulgence (and the rumor during the revolutionary reign of terror in Paris that pregnant women would not be guillotined contributed to an element of promiscuity in the crowded prisons of the French capital). But the views and campaigns of the feminist pioneers attracted little attention and less sympathy at the time. They did, however, lay the groundwork for what would later develop into a campaign and charter for feminine rights, sexual and otherwise.

During the nineteenth century, continuing social turbulence was nourished by the consequences of industrialization and the explosive expansion of cities. Unemployment and grinding poverty in those cities resulted in the development of active and violent criminality and growing disrespect for authority among ever-increasing numbers of poor, hopeless people. Already recoiling against revolutionary license which gnawed at their ordered picture of the universe, the middle classes, growing in affluence and influence, were prodded into a determined search for stability and security, in the realm of personal behavior as well as in society generally.

Rigid standards of morality were imposed which, among other things, sought to suppress the threatening implications of erotic permissiveness. It did this by trying to turn sexual pleasure into loathsome degeneracy. An obsession with feminine "purity" developed. Bizarre efforts were made to shield females from erotic reference, suggestion or thought. Thomas Bowdler's antiseptic *Family Shakespeare*, which omitted words and passages of Shakespeare's plays "which cannot with propriety be read aloud in a family," was reissued regularly throughout the period and sold well. Girls were kept so ignorant of the physiological implications of sexuality that their first mysterious menstrual experiences baffled and frightened them, sometimes provoking hysteria. Without going into what they considered squalid detail, mothers cautioned daughters – who had been taught distaste for, and fear of, sex – to tolerate the unseemly developments that awaited them on their wedding nights. For many, the experience must have been emotionally and physically traumatic.

Women blushed at the vaguest sexual references and could be expected to swoon at anything even bordering on the specific. Indeed, such blushings and swoonings were the mark of a respectable female. Medical offices came equipped with dummies on which women could indicate where their own bodies were subject to pain or discomfort so that doctors would not be required to take excessive liberties when examining female patients. Female bodies were sealed in petticoats, long dresses and high stockings. Exposure of so much as an unclothed woman's ankle was extremely immodest and was believed to be capable of unleashing fantasies of carnal desire in the minds of otherwise respectable men.

As for men, they were generally allowed a greater measure of sexual freedom – but not always. Provided they were discreet, men could maintain secret liaisons, whether in brothels

153

or through other arrangements. The novelist Samuel Butler, who hinted at his own unhappy sex life in his partly autobiographical novel *The Way of All Flesh*, made discreet weekly Wednesday mid-afternoon visits to a woman in north London and afterward left behind one pound for her services each time. (Butler recommended her to a friend who did the same, on Tuesdays.)

But in proper English middle-class society, dread of sexual indulgence was so drummed into the heads of boys that one distinguished general later recalled how, at the age of fourteen, he had wished he was a eunuch. An obsessive fear of masturbation plagued parents and schools. Boys were warned it could cause amnesia, tuberculosis, blindness, curvature of the spine, insanity and other misfortunes. Contraptions were devised for affixing to the penis at night to prevent boys from abusing themselves. Even more inventive were devices to guard men against involuntary nocturnal emissions. These included a contraption with metal edges which was strapped to the male genital area at night. If the penis erected while the man was sleeping, he was awakened by the jab of metal against it. He was then to remove the device, soak his offending organ in cold water till it subsided, affix the apparatus to his genitals again and go back to innocent sleep.

A German doctor, despairing of masculine self-control and deeply concerned about the dangers of population explosion, recommended the application of a metal seal within the penis itself to prevent sexual intercourse:

The foreskin is drawn forward and gently compressed between a pair of perforated metal plates so that when a hollow needle, containing a core of lead wire is stuck through it, it is hardly felt. When the wire has been drawn through, it is bent so that it cannot press on the adjacent parts. Both ends are now brought together and soldered together with a small soldering rod. As soon as the knot, the size of a pea, has cooled off, a solid object is held against it; a small metal seal is pressed on it and this is afterwards kept in safety. This makes it impossible to

154

open the infibulation and afterwards close it without being discovered. . . .

In the obscurantist Middle Ages or during the subsequent witchcraft craze, such a device might have been policed by dedicated public guardians, acting with religious conviction and fervor. But despite the depth and breadth of nineteenth-century puritanism, middle-class propriety was commonly mocked both by neglect and open defiance, even by prominent public personalities. King Ludwig I of Bavaria made no secret of taking Lola Montez (Dublin-born Marie Dolores Gilbert) as his mistress, despite her many earlier affairs, including those with Franz Liszt and Alexander Dumas. Little effort was made to conceal the fact that the English actress Henrietta Howard was mistress of Napoleon III. Lillie Langtry, another English beauty, numbered a king of Belgium, a crown prince of Austria, a Texas cattle baron and a Prince of Wales among her lovers. The philandering Prince of Wales was, incidentally, publicly implicated in a divorce case, prompting his mother, Queen Victoria, to regret that he had been damaged "in the eyes of the middle and lower classes, which is to be lamented in these days when the higher classes, in their frivolities, selfish and self-seeking lives, do more to increase the spirit of democracy than anything else."

The nineteenth century was a golden age of prostitution. Cities and city populations expanded at a feverish pace under the impact of the industrial revolution. The populations of whores expanded accordingly to meet the demand for their services (and to provide a precarious living for countless women who would otherwise have had no means of support). At mid-century, there were 43,000 registered (and even more unregistered) whores in Paris, which then had a population of less than a million. In London, although Victorian prudishness was much more in evidence there, the proportion was almost as high. Prostitutes were among the hordes of new arrivals who transformed San Francisco from a sleepy village into a boom town within weeks in 1849 after gold had been discovered nearby.

155

The profession was as rigidly stratified as it had been in ancient Greece. At the top were the queens of the *demi-monde*, often women who had risen, by virtue of their looks, skills and ambition, from humble origins to become celebrated international courtesans, pursued by kings and millionaires. Giulia Benini, an Italian who conquered Paris with her beauty and explosive temperament and was luxuriously quartered in a Champs-Elysées apartment, was said to include almost the entire diplomatic corps in the French capital among her lovers. In London, crowds would gather along Rotten Row in Hyde Park where the most eminent and beautiful courtesans of the city would make appearances on horseback at fixed times each day – it was one of the major sights of the city and an important social occasion for the women themselves. Cora Pearl, who was English, became notorious in France for her ability to win the affections of the husbands of even the most beautiful women there, specializing in royalty and aristocracy. At one point, Count Napoleon Daru, who dabbled in politics, shared her services with his son, Viscount Paul Daru. In New York, journals like the *Scorpion* titillated their readers with accounts of the illicit affairs of prominent men and tantalizing courtesans.

The next stratum of prostitutes were the women and girls who worked in brothels. Many of these were fashionable establishments, frequented by wealthy merchants and professional men and by gentry without sufficient resources to support private courtesans. Some in Paris – like those at 6 Rue des Moulins and 13 Rue St. Augustin – had international reputations and clienteles. They were lavishly appointed and were visited as regularly by many of their clients as nightclubs were later to be frequented, with the difference that there was no need to bring along female companions. So lucrative was the high-class brothel trade that the Everleigh sisters, originally from Louisville, Kentucky, seeking a safe investment for some money they had acquired, opened a splendorous whorehouse in Omaha, Nebraska toward the end of the century and made a fortune from it.

Less luxurious were the whorehouses which attracted a less

affluent clientele. In France, as the short stories of de Maupassant testify, this sort of brothel was an unpretentious social center, a carefree meeting place for respectable local merchants and professional men, a place for them to relax. Similar establishments existed in other countries, often perhaps without the *savoir faire* which the Gallic imagination provided.

The whores who worked in them could only hope to put by enough savings (or perhaps even capture a husband) before being compelled by the ravages of age to slip down a rung in the ladder and find a place in less cheering or less stable surroundings, in working-class district brothels where brief, cold sexual servicing was generally their only function. Such places flourished in port-cities and back streets of urban clusters as far back as history goes. A French visitor to New York at the turn of the nineteenth century reported that he had found whole streets there given over to such brothels. In 1880, it was calculated there was one prostitute for every fifteen adult males in New York.

There were rigid distinctions among free-lance prostitutes as well. Those who frequented theaters in search of clients – well-dressed, well-poised females, comfortable in such surroundings – looked haughtily down on those who loitered on the pavement outside and nearby. And prostitutes who paraded their wares in broad daylight even in disreputable sections of town looked down on those who worked there at night, vast numbers of them driven into squalid whoredom by the vicious poverty that was a by-product of nineteenth-century economic progress.

It was these last who swelled the ranks of the whores to barely credible numbers, seeking some means of survival at a time of social upheaval. An Edinburgh medical journal reported in 1859:

Let anyone walk certain streets of London, Glasgow or Edinburgh of a night and, without troubling his head with statistics, his eyes and ears will tell him at once what a multitudinous amazonian army the devil keeps in constant field service for advancing his own ends. The stones seem alive with lust . . .

The name "hooker," meaning whore, derives from the camp followers who clustered around the troops of General Joseph Hooker, stationed in Washington during the American Civil War.

The steady spread of literacy and the development of improved printing techniques enormously expanded the market for and means of disseminating erotic literature. As has already been suggested, so did society's attempts to impose puritanical restraints. The range of sexually descriptive and sexually titillating writings was enormous. It included the first pornographic magazines, exposés of real or fabricated sex scandals, and tales of seduction and sexual adventure. There were also sex manuals and serious novels which, despite prevailing blinkers, dared to presume there were such things as prostitutes and sex-hungry men and women. There was erotic verse, like this anonymous sonnet quoted in Ronald Pearsall's *The Worm in the Bud*:

> *Ye Gods! the raptures of that night!*
> *What fierce convulsions of delight!*
> *How in each other's arms involv'd,*
> *We lay confounded, and dissolv'd!*
> *Bodies mingling, sexes blending,*
> *Which should most be lost contending;*
> *Darting fierce, and flaming kisses,*
> *Plunging into boundless blisses;*
> *Our bodies and our souls on fire,*
> *Tost by a tempest of desire;*
> *'Till with the utmost fury dow'n,*
> *Down, at once, we sunk to heav'n.*

My Secret Life, eleven volumes in all, was the anonymous work of a sex fanatic whose entire life had seemingly been centered on seduction and copulation. *The Ups and Downs of Life*, by Edward Sellon, was an autobiography of an imaginative, intelligent man whose definition of power and pleasure was apparently related exclusively to the sexual possession of women.

There was a host of less comprehensive and considerably less ambitious works, slight erotic fantasies : *A Night in a Moorish Harem* (the story of a British naval officer who has the run of a pasha's wives' quarters one night), *Adventures of a Lady's Maid, Venus in Boston, The Amatory Adventures of Tilly Touchitt, A Young Wife's Confession, The Lady Libertine* – the list was immense, the market apparently insatiable.

There was a spate of "how-to" books. These included such manuals as *The Art of Kissing in All its Varieties, The Art of Making Love in More Ways Than One*, and *The Delights of Love. Every Woman's Book*, published in England in 1826, listed various contraceptive methods, including the use of sheaths, *coitus interruptus* and a vaginal sponge (noting the practice of a female aristocrat who was said never to go out to dinner without being prepared with a sponge). A *Private Companion to Young Married People*, published in America in 1832, also detailed advisable contraceptive precautions and obviously was not meant only for those safely joined in marriage. A popular French sex manual dealt with different approaches men should employ for women who were easily aroused and those who were not.

Perhaps most fascinating was the scholarship which suddenly was devoted to erotic literature by a number of learned individuals. Henry Spencer Ashbee compiled a monumental three-volume bibliography of erotic literature titled *Index Librorum Prohibitorum* and published it under the pseudonym "Pisanus Fraxi." Through the title, Ashbee was both mocking the *Catholic Index of Prohibited Books*, which bore the same Latin title, and conferring a deserved aura of scholarship on his work. Another Englishman, John Davenport, produced *Curiositates Eroticae Physiologiae. A Bibliographie Erotique* appeared in France and similar compilations were put together in Germany.

Non-erotic literature also often served to widen the sexual imagination of the period. Tolstoy's *Anna Karenina* and

Flaubert's *Madam Bovary* showed how sexual involvement could ruin respectable women. Anna's passionate, ultimately tragic, affair with Vronsky had an appealing, romantic power which many less daring Victorian women must have found enchanting. Kate Chopin, an American novelist, was among a growing number of writers whose works portrayed women who defied conventional restraints and who were prepared to enjoy sex with neither matrimonial attachments nor romantic illusions.

Novels by Zola and Dostoevsky portrayed prostitutes as sympathetic beings, as did Bret Harte's famous California gold rush story, *The Outcasts of Poker Flat*. Frank Wedekind's plays in Germany, notably *Spring Awakening*, about adolescent sexuality, openly explored erotic themes. A stage was being set for the emergence in our own times of a body of literature in which the distinct line between erotic and non-erotic fiction would either vanish or become irrelevant.

The pattern of erotic art also underwent marked alterations during the nineteenth century. The most notable innovations during the early part of the period were characterized by a bawdy playfulness, notably in the works of Thomas Rowlandson, or a sense of mystery, such as was conveyed in the works of Henry Fuseli.

The sketches of Rowlandson cut through the pretentious, overblown etiquette of proper society. They had more to do with a roll in the hay than with courtly finesse or sly middle-class shenanigans. His images of copulating couples, many with lewd grins plastered across their faces, allow for no romantic illusions whatsoever. One sketch pictures a couple copulating perpendicularly in a graveyard amidst ironically emblazoned tombstones – one marked with crossed penises, another bearing the legend, "Here lies entombed . . . the scabbard of ten thousand pricks." Fuseli's dream-like images – like that in his painting of *Lady Betty*, which shows a woman holding a disembodied penis – was a haunting prelude to the Freudian impact, still the better part of a century away.

While encompassing new aesthetic horizons, the erotic

imagery of the late nineteenth century, when Victorian prudery was at its height, intriguingly borrowed some of its thrust
from the antiseptic romanticism on which sexual repression
was based. There was a profound earnestness to the captivating nudes of such masters as Ingres, Courbet, Manet, Alma-
Tadema, Leighton, Millet and Poynter. The American sculptor Hiram Powers gained momentary fame for his depiction
of naked female beauty in his statue of *The Greek Slave*,
rendered with the same earnestness as painters of the period.
It was as if worship of the female form, implying as it did
conscious transgression of Victorian taboos, ruled out both a
less somber vision and sheer fun. Like many revolutionaries,
these artists were so committed that they could not gauge the
degree of their humorlessness, or the degree to which they
were governed by what they were committed against.

As the century drew to a close, however, the heavy weight of
erotic sobriety grew too much to bear and was shunted aside
by a new school of illustrators, the most prominent of whom
was Aubrey Beardsley. Though he died at the age of twenty-
six (in 1898), Beardsley's erotic vision captured a provocative,
much less self-important, intensely erotic imagery. His drawings, especially those which illustrated Oscar Wilde's *Salome*
and an edition of *Lysistrata*, conveyed a mixture of levity and
the macabre, mystery and mockery, highlighted by a focus on,
among other things, gargantuan penises and formidable
naked behinds. Though shunned for his "obscene" creations,
Beardsley's work – like the erotic poems of Baudelaire and
other writers of the so-called decadent movement – could not
be dismissed. It served notice that once again, elements of the
popular image of sexual indulgence were arriving on the
scene and would not be suppressed.

Solid citizens, convinced that all questions had already been
answered ("God's in his heaven, All's right with the world!"),
were baffled and confounded by developments which dis-
turbed their complacency. They were outraged by Charles
Darwin's suggestions about their simian ancestry. Karl Marx
and others were devising critiques and analyses of the

dynamic forces in society and plotting utopias which had nothing to do with etiquette or the kingdom of heaven. Sigmund Freud was beginning his explorations into the human psyche and others had already played around the fringes of that same unnerving terrain.

The French psychologist Alfred Binet, better known for his study of ways of testing intelligence, suggested that sexual fetishes (Binet coined the expression), in which individuals were erotically aroused by normally non-sexual phenomena, could be explained through an understanding of what those individuals saw or otherwise experienced, and to which they became "fixated" during their earliest sexual awakenings. Among the fetish cases which neurologist Jean Charcot, who specialized in hysteria and who numbered Freud among his students, described was one in which a young boy happened for the first time to have become conscious of his erection at the exact moment when he observed a grown-up member of his family putting on his night cap before going to sleep. He next felt sexual excitement when seeing an elderly female retainer adjust her night cap. By the time he himself was an adult, he had developed a fetish which required him to imagine his wife as an old woman in a night cap before being able to copulate with her.

Though purporting to stick to the facts, the new scientific approach to an analysis of sexual motives and behavior produced quite as many generalities as more obscurantist earlier periods. Austrian psychiatrist Richard Krafft-Ebing, for example, pronounced, "if a woman is normally developed mentally and well-bred, her sexual desire is small. If this were not so, the whole world would become a brothel, and marriage and a family impossible."

Abnormality was Krafft-Ebing's speciality. He compiled *Psychopathia Sexualis* in which he dealt extensively with deviant sexual practices and fetishes and thereby blazed a path in scholarship which twentieth-century sex researchers, though discarding most of his conclusions, would follow. Among the deviant behavior patterns upon which Krafft-Ebing cast light was that which involved deriving sexual pleasure from being abused and physically beaten. Masochism, he called it, after the Austrian writer Leopold von Sacher-Masoch who wrote stories about men who delighted in being beaten by women, and who himself shared that strange delight.

Flagellation was known as "the English disease" because of the frequency with which it was encountered in Britain. Some attributed this craving for beating and being beaten as a means of achieving sexual fulfillment to the experiences of flagellation many English boys went through, notably in such distinguished public schools as Eton where in times past younger boys were regularly whipped, often for the slightest transgressions. In addition to the pain, those beaten were accorded at least temporary respect, sympathy and status by other boys in a rigid, frigid environment in which it was common for older and stronger boys to bully younger and weaker ones heartlessly. For many, it had lasting consequences.

Many London brothels specialized in flagellation, keeping elaborate chains, whips and other devices of punishment available to service those who found erotic satisfaction in pain. They numbered among their clients many eminent politicians and aristocrats, some of whom required that they be treated like schoolboys who had misbehaved. Rider Haggard's novel *She* ("who must be obeyed"), a mysterious, alluring, all-powerful white goddess figure in Africa, probably owed some of its enormous success to the obedience-punishment overtones it manifested.

Flagellants were divided into three categories: those who wanted to be severely beaten by women who took pleasure (or pretended to take pleasure) from wielding the rod; those who preferred to whip others; and those who wanted only to watch while others were being beaten. A London banker was reported to have made an arrangement with two girls' schools which provided him with peep holes through which he could secretly watch girls being whipped for misbehaving.

Americans, still exotic creatures to many Europeans but already credited with technological ingenuity, were said at the time to have invented automated flagellation. They were

163

reported – falsely, but to the admiration of some – to have contrived an automatic whipping device in which the masochist could adjust himself into place to be whipped mechanically, a unique form of masturbation.

The development of standards of acceptable sexual behavior in America – like so many things American – was baffling to European observers. Even after the puritan ethic of colonial times had been tempered and transformed, a potent residual aversion to erotic indulgence pervaded respectable society in the United States. Females went to great lengths to make themselves alluring, but prevailing moral indoctrination directed their appetites away from sensual gratification, and this peculiarity tended to be honored by males.

A British visitor commented admiringly that a pretty young lady could travel alone "with perfect safety from Maine to Missouri and will meet with nothing but respect and attention the whole way." Stendhal was astonished by what he saw: "At Boston, a girl can be left perfectly safely with a handsome stranger – in all probability she is thinking of nothing but her marriage settlement."

The way was prepared for the sexless American beauties of the twentieth century for whom looking desirable was to be the prime goal of existence (involving incessant cosmetic artifice), but for whom sexual indulgence would be an intolerable violation, involving as it did the messing of hairdos and the smearing of lipstick. Most remarkable in this development was the acceptance by so many American males of a passive role in (very limited) sexual relations (and in husband-wife relations) while continuing to exercise an unrelentingly dominant role in all other matters. Visiting the United States in the 1860s, English novelist Anthony Trollope objected bitterly:

[American women] have no scruple at demanding from men everything that a man can be called on to relinquish on a woman's behalf, but they do so without any of that grace which turns the demand into a favor conferred.

164

The frontier mentality, which was immensely influential in shaping American attitudes, may have been responsible. As Americans (and new arrivals from abroad) moved westward across the continent from one often precarious frontier to another during the nineteenth century, they had to cope with a serious shortage of women required to perform natural and commonly accepted feminine functions – procreating, child-rearing, house-tending, husband-comforting, teaching and generally bringing a measure of civilization to the untamed prairies and fledgling settlements. Men outnumbered women three-to-one in California in 1860. There were twenty men to every woman in Colorado at the time. As railroad links spread, men were heard to say they would "marry any female getting off the train." The result was that, on the frontier, women tended to be accorded an exaggerated respect and deference that the desperate need for them evoked.

They, in turn, stepped gracefully onto the pedestal fashioned by that need. Many frontier attitudes became part of the "American ethic." To the often cowed American male, mother, wife, even girl friend became formidable personalities, to be catered for, listened to, obeyed – much more so than anywhere else in the world. It accounts perhaps for the fact that women's liberation campaigns have been far more vigorous and successful in America than anywhere else. It accounts also for the fact that legend pictures two primary females in the American West of the nineteenth century – the reliable, invincible Earth Mother type and the warm-hearted, expendable whore.

From *Manual of Classical Erotology*, **by Friedrich K. Forberg**

.... I was naked; his member stood straight up. He immediately placed his hands on my breasts and brandishing his inflamed lance between my thighs, he said, "See, madam, how this weapon darts at you, not to threaten you, but to give you the greatest possible pleasure. Pray, guide this blind applicant into the dark recess, so that it may not miss its destination. I will not remove my hands from where they are. I would not deprive them of the bliss they enjoy." I do as he wishes. I introduce the flaming dart into the burning center. He feels it, pushes and throngs in. . . . After one or two strokes, I am melting with incredible titillation. . . . "Stop," I cried. "Stop my soul. It is escaping!" "I know," he replied, laughing, "from where. Your soul wants to escape through this lower orifice of which I have taken possession. But I keep it well stoppered." Whilst speaking, he endeavored, by holding his breath, still to increase the already enormous size of his swollen member. "I am going to thrust back your escaping soul", he added, lunging at me more violently. . . . Doubling his strokes, he filled me with such a delicious transport that although he could not get his whole body into me, he impregnated me with all his passion, all his lascivious desire, his very thoughts, his whole delirious soul, his voluptuous embraces.

From *The Sexual Relations of Mankind*, **by Paolo Mantegazza (1831-1910)**

We are a modest and, above all, a hypocritical people. We have learned to blush at the mere sight of a pair of underpants or at the sound of certain words which we carefully guard between the moldy pages of specialized dictionaries. We hold no festivals to honor the appearance of the God of Love, no rights of consecration. Often, parents do not even know that their own son has graduated to manhood, that their own daughter has become a woman. The laundress claims possession of that secret. She laughs over it and gossips about it with the chambermaid or the cook. What we have are lascivious frenzies, nocturnal self-communions, with the silence of dark corridors and cellars to hide the emergence of the force that is meant to transform and redouble life, as if it were a crime. . . .

The principal causes of polygamy and polyandry are an exaggerated fondness for variety and a pride in owning what others do not possess. The need for variety is such that often the worse is preferred only because it is different from the better. The curiosity that was Eve's downfall is still one of the most fertile sources of sin. . . . Polygamy and polyandry, which originate in the deepest wellsprings of human nature, could become social institutions, sanctioned by law.

From *The Functions and Disorders of the Reproductive Organs,*
by Dr. William Acton

We find . . . that some men reach adult age without having experienced any sexual desire at all. That complete sexual quiescence which we have noticed as being the proper condition of childhood continues in such cases during the period of youth, extending even into adult age. In some it is only at an abnormally late period that the natural sexual desire commences. . . . [This condition] occurs principally where the intellectual powers have been very highly cultivated or where the body has been subjected to strong and constant physical exertion. . . . A large class of men commonly supposed to be nervous, bashful or timid are in fact sufferers from this absence of sexual feeling, which may, perhaps, be due to their having been brought up in retired country places without any female companions. They can hardly be said to have lost that of which they had never had experience, or to have failed to exercise powers of whose very existence they are unconscious. . . . It would be obviously erroneous to conclude without further evidence that any individual of this class is in fact impotent, when all that can be said of him is that his life has been perfectly chaste, and undisturbed by the usual virile phenomenon.

From *The Kama Sutra* of **Vatsyayana**

(Written in India in the fourth century and translated into English
by Sir Richard Burton (1821-1890).)

While the woman is lying on his bed, and is as it were abstracted by his conversation, [the man] should loosen the knot of her undergarments, and when she begins to dispute with him, he should overwhelm her with kisses. Then when his lingam is erect he should touch her with his hands in various places and gently manipulate various parts of her body. If the woman is bashful, and if it is the first time that they have come together, the man should place his hands between her thighs which she would probably keep close together, and if she is a very young girl, he should first get his hands upon her breasts which she would probably cover with her own hands, and under her armpits and on her neck. If however she is a seasoned woman, he should do whatever is agreeable either to him or to her, and whatever is fitting for the occasion. . . . He should gather from the action of the woman what things would be pleasing to her during congress. . . .

From *Psychopathia Sexualis*, **by Richard Krafft-Ebing**

The propagation of the human race is not left to mere accident or the caprices of the individual, but is guaranteed by the hidden laws of nature which are enforced by a mighty, irresistible impulse. Sensual enjoyment and physical fitness are not the only conditions for the enforcement of these laws, but higher motives and aims, such as the desire to continue the species or the individuality of mental and physical qualities beyond time and space, exert considerable influence. Man puts himself at once on a level with the beast if he seeks to gratify lust alone, but he elevates his superior position when by curbing the animal desire he combines with the sexual functions ideas of morality, of the sublime, and the beautiful. . . . If man were deprived of sexual distinction and the nobler enjoyments arising therefrom, all poetry and probably all moral tendency would be eliminated from his life. Sexual life no doubt is the one mighty factor in the individual and social relations of man which discloses his powers of activity, of acquiring property, of establishing a home, of awakening altruistic sentiments toward a person of the opposite sex, and toward his own issue as well as towards the whole human race.

From *Leaves of Grass*, by Walt Whitman

A woman waits for me, she contains all, nothing is lacking,
Yet all were lacking if sex were lacking, or if the moisture of the right
*   man were lacking.*

Sex contains all, bodies, souls,
Meanings, proofs, purities, delicacies, results, promulgations,
Songs, commands, health, pride, the maternal mystery, the seminal
*   milk,*
All hopes, benefactions, bestowals, all the passions, loves, beauties,
*   delights of the earth,*
All the governments, judges, gods, follow'd persons of the earth,
These are contain'd in sex as parts of itself and justifications of itself.

Without shame the man I like knows and avows the deliciousness of his
*   sex,*
Without shame the woman I like knows and avows hers.

Now I will dismiss myself from impassive women,
I will go stay with her who waits for me, and with those women that are
*   warm-blooded and sufficient for me,*
I see that they understand me and do not deny me,
I see that they are worthy of me, I will be the robust husband of those
*   women.*

171

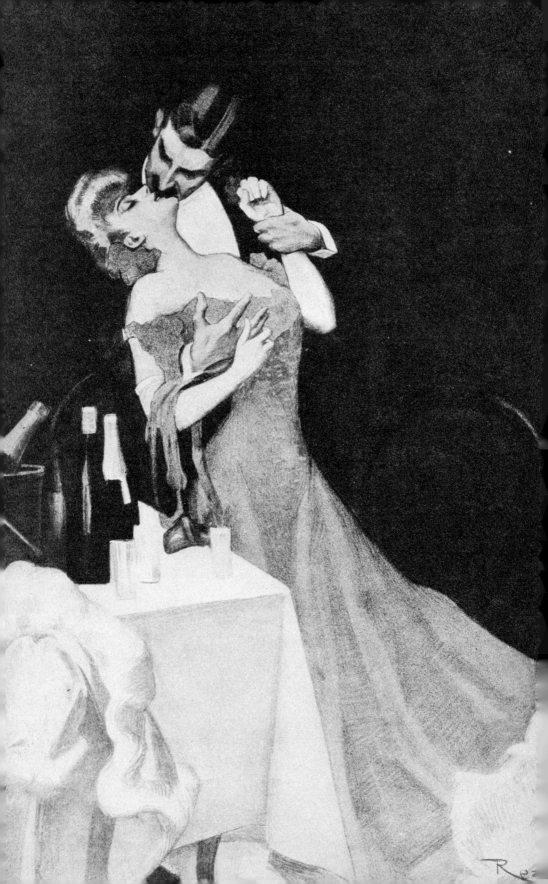

Eros Triumphant

Eros Triumphant

*If fucking is a bad thing then so are we; there is no hope, because what
makes us bad is what makes us.*

— WAYLAND YOUNG, *Eros Denied*

NOT FOR MILLIONS of years have there been such colossal
developments in human sexuality as right now. The implications for sexual behavior have not been so formidable since
our primitive ancestors evolved into *homo sapiens* — not since
they adjusted their sexual equipment so that men and women
could copulate face-to-face; not since the human female
became sexually receptive the year round.

Limited sexual seasons in other animals served to control
their numbers. But woman's year-round sexual receptivity
allowed for no such in-built control in humans. It posed a
danger of exposing females of child-bearing age to virtually
perpetual pregnancy. Aside from reducing them to the status
of machines endlessly churning out babies, it would have
presented a serious threat of rapid, disastrous over-
population.

This threat was averted through astoundingly effective
devices which emerged in the evolution of human society.
These devices included sexual modesty, sexual taboos, religious sexual prohibitions and restraints, and other restrictive codes which quickly became crucial elements of family
and community life.

Though reasonably effective in limiting population growth,
protecting the family unit and promoting harmonious community development, sexual restraints failed to resolve an

174

unyielding conundrum: they remained restrictive – sometimes more, sometimes less – despite the fact that sexual activity never became less physically pleasurable or less exciting. For social reasons (to live together and work together), we taught ourselves to curb our sexual impulse. As Sigmund Freud put it, "Civilization is built upon renunciation of instinctual gratification."

But times have changed. Some things which were once important are now, at best, peripheral. Herbert Marcuse has noted that, "The inevitable decline in the need for work in modern society renders Freud's identification of civilization with sexual repression no longer valid. When work is no longer necessary, neither is sexual repression." In fact, sexual repression began declining sharply in our society long before the arrival of the no-need-for-work utopia – for several reasons.

The development of readily available contraceptives, particularly "the pill," has had a serious impact on sexual standards. Various surveys provide the evidence. A recent study, for example, indicated that nearly one-third of teenaged American girls had experienced sexual intercourse. That points to a 30 percent increase in female adolescent sexual participation in the United States, without a corresponding increase in illegitimate births, in six short years ending in 1977, at a time when popular use of medically prescribed contraceptives was still a comparatively recent development! An innovation for which the world had been waiting, it caught on very fast.

No less significant has been the crusade to end the historic subservience of women. The campaign, an outgrowth of nineteenth-century women's liberation agitation (which, in turn, had its origins in earlier feminist eruptions), has met with varying degrees of success in more affluent parts of the world. Among other things, it has gained for women some of the sexual freedom that has, in the past, usually been men's exclusive preserve.

Less monumental but still of considerable significance in the modern sexual environment has been the increasingly publicized search for personal fulfillment through sexual satisfaction. For the first time in history, deliberate sexual questing is not confined primarily to men of privileged social classes. The orgasm has become an object of conscious pursuit for millions of men and women. There is an ever-growing library of manuals which describe ways in which the search for it can be painlessly pursued. The *New York Times* called *The Joy of Sex* by Alex Comfort "the most widely used 'how-to' book of the '70s" – a remarkable tribute in this age of do-it-yourself frenzy.

The permissive, even frantic sexual climate has inevitably supported and encouraged a massive dissemination of erotica (though there are those who insist it is the other way round). Movie pictures, one of the major cultural innovations of the twentieth century, became a prime medium for sexually provocative themes. Films with specifically erotic orientation gained huge audiences despite residual popular feelings that casual, easily accessible pornography should not be encouraged. A Swedish movie exploring sexual experimentation in the 1960s, *I am Curious Yellow*, was one of the earliest to gain wide distribution and, to the horror of moralists, taught a lesson to the makers of other movies by earning at the box office more than fifty times what it cost to make. Sexually arousing themes and images on television reached far larger audiences than erotica had ever reached before, and it reached them in their cosy family environments, making at least the milder forms of sexual arousal seem the most natural thing in the world.

In the United States, a congressionally-appointed committee reported in 1970, "Approximately 85% of adult men and 70% of adult women . . . have been exposed at some time during their lives to depictions of explicit sexual material in either visual or textual form." Even before the report was published, the pace of the times had made its conclusions an underestimate.

Sexually provocative popular songs "turned on" youngsters around the world. *Wake Up and Make Love With Me* purred pop singer Ian Dury. *I Can't Get No Satisfaction* screeched the sensually gyrating lead singer of the internationally-acclaimed Rolling Stones pop group and the cheers could have drowned out the din of an earthquake.

Photos of voluptuous females appeared regularly in popular newspapers for no other reason than their sexual glitter – a daily topless page-three pinup helped the *Sun* become Britain's largest circulation daily within a few years of its inception. Girlie magazines attracted mass readerships – *Playboy* leading the field with a mixture of sex and culture. Other magazines chose less culture and more explicit titles, like *Orgy* and *Screw*, to attract readers. England's Bishop of Woolwich declared, "There is nothing obscene whatever in the portrayal, however explicit, of the erotic as such. The erotic is something to be enjoyed." And more and more people were enjoying it.

Fashions in clothes reflected the twentieth century's erotic atmosphere. They featured such sexually revealing fads as tight sweaters for buxom females, "falsies" for females who weren't buxom but wanted to be; abbreviated "hot pants" which covered little beneath the thigh and equally revealing mini-skirts; see-through blouses; tight trousers which clung almost as closely as skin to the contours of the body.

"Wife-swap" clubs were formed in the 1960s for married couples who wished to legitimize and facilitate extramarital sexual adventure. A 1970's New York "swing-club" developed a new form of orgy: couples arrived together, paid admission at the door and, along with dozens of other couples, put on displays of copulation (the copulating couples were often not those who arrived together) or simply watched other club members copulating. (Thirty years earlier, a public opinion poll had indicated that "the average American" thought women petted and kissed too much before marriage.)

In some places, sexual activity in public became for a time a symbol of a new dimension of personal freedom. In Spain, the overthrow of a puritanical dictatorship was followed by exhibitions of public copulation by youngsters – they outraged their elders, both with their shamelessness and their ability to go

177

unpunished. In libertarian Holland, where such flauntings occurred earlier than in most places, older travelers protested in vain about the habit of young couples of copulating in moving passenger trains, regardless and oblivious of the presence of others.

Sex boutiques have sprung up in major western cities. They offer a range of sex aids, including dildoes, French ticklers (rubbery devices for affixing to the penis to tickle vagina walls), woman-sized rubber dolls with vagina and mouth openings, vibrators, "instant erection" lotions, sexual lubricants and various alleged aphrodisiacs. A new breed of consultant – sexual therapists – emerged to help those who had difficulty indulging in sexual activity or enjoying it as much as they thought they should.

The ages of erotica and commercialism coincided and it was inevitable that sexual imagery would be exploited in advertising, to peddle goods which had nothing to do with sex. Whether it was for soap or cigarettes, cars or clothes, whether in print, on television or on billboards, advertisements featuring sexually desirable women and men were effective in promoting the sale of products. One critic complained in 1972, "Obscene words and phrases are now an inescapable part of the flotsam and jetsam of today's admass argot of communications." Regardless how farfetched, associating a product with sexual promise proved a winning sales argument. Some countries, seeking to discourage cigarette smoking for health reasons, acknowledged the success of sex-linked ads by banning their use in cigarette advertising.

Like everything else, prostitution altered its pattern to fit the modern age. Around 1900, a significant change in brothel logistics had occurred with the establishment in Paris of so-called *maisons des rendezvous* where prostitutes worked but did not live. Whores became employed at their jobs as others were at theirs. Later in the century, vacation visits to Manila whorehouses – unblushingly organized like ordinary package tours – were to be arranged for Tokyo businessmen. A group of housewives in New York's suburbia were discovered to have turned to occasional prostitution to break the tedium of their lives and earn a few extra dollars. Hamburg had its modern, elaborate "Eros Centers" of prostitution. Respectable tourist guides to Amsterdam pinpointed the city's redlight district in which clever lighting patterns and picture windows were utilized to display the carnal attributes of prostitutes to passers-by in the street.

Prostitutes in San Francisco, and later in London and various other places, formed organizations to protect the rights and interests of the working whore. Massage parlors, most of them barely disguised brothels, sprang up in the center of major American cities, and in other parts of the world as well. Many street-walking whores in Italy and France, and elsewhere, tired of the pedestrian life and took to cruising around in automobiles to find their clients, pulling over to the curb to solicit them. In virtually all parts of the western world, prostitutes advertised, placing ads in magazines and newspapers and, especially in Europe, putting notices in candy store card-display windows, alongside those advertising plumbers and babysitters. A cascade of sociological studies of the motives and habits of prostitutes (and their clients) lent some of them an aura of normalcy and usefulness they had never fully enjoyed since the days of ancient Greece. Freud, for example, asserted:

> Full sexual satisfaction can only come for [middle-class man] when he can give himself up whole-heartedly to enjoyment which, with his well-brought-up wife, for instance, he does not venture to do. Hence comes his need for a less exalted sexual object, a woman ethically inferior, to whom he need ascribe no aesthetic misgivings and who does not know about the rest of his life and cannot criticize him.

A book written by a prostitute (*The Happy Hooker*) and another by a "madam" (*A House Is Not a Home*) were critically acclaimed and became best-sellers.

Even before the erotic climate had grown so pervasive, the

absurdities and inadequacies of Victorian prohibitions had been generally recognized. Prevailing moral codes had begun to change. For example, Victorian strictures against husbands and wives enjoying each other sexually (rather than just making babies) became untenable even for the most puritanical. Early in this century, carnal bliss outside matrimonial union continued to be seen by guardians of public morals as a danger to society, a violation of religious law and a corrupter of children. But even before the "flapper" age of the 1920s, with its free love philosophy captivating both intellectual rebels and hedonists, sexual pleasure was generally deemed permissible, even commendable, if nuptial and private.

Thus, the Dutch gynecologist Theodore van de Velde became internationally famous with the publication in the 1920s of his book *Ideal Marriage*. Van de Velde set out to instruct husbands and wives how best to achieve sexual fulfillment with each other:

> In practiced lovers, especially between partners who have become thoroughly adapted to each other's individualities, both preliminary prelude and love play may be "got through" in one brief gesture, or wholly dispensed with. A look, a word of invitation and suggestion suffice. . . . But this lightning love contact can only occur very seldom and on exceptional occasions between persons of finer feelings and only such are capable of Ideal Marriage. . . . For the man who neglects love play is guilty not only of coarseness but of positive brutality; and his omission can not only offend and disgust a woman, but also injure her on the purely physical plane.

Van de Velde went into detail on suggested forms of love play, the various forms of kissing, different postures of copulation. His message reflected a general revulsion against the grotesque priggishness of Victorian morals. But this reaction had implications far beyond the confines of matrimony. If respectable society could applaud the transformation of husbands and wives into each other's lovers, sexual pleasure could no longer be dismissed as wicked in itself. As a consequence, condemnation of sex even outside marriage, of casual sexual adventure, of promiscuity and of general erotic display gradually grew to be seen as cranky and became decreasingly effective.

The distribution of pornographic literature had already broadened meaningfully. Shortly before the outbreak of the First World War, an English clergyman complained, ". . . this erotic contemptible trash has great vogue with the idle classes. . . . These corrosive novels are flaunted beneath the eyes of a passing public in the most seductive guise. One of the worst of them . . . came out magnificently apparelled in royal purple and coroneted. A lady found it on a railway bookstall which she believed was impeccable and because she had just re-papered her bedrooms with the same royal purple, purchased five of the beastly books right off and put one in each said bedroom."

Serious writers explored the sexual terrain in works which were much more than merely erotic – D.H. Lawrence in *Lady Chatterley's Lover*, Radclyffe Hall in *The Well of Loneliness*, James Joyce in *Ulysses*, James Farrell in *Studs Lonigan*, Erskine Caldwell in *God's Little Acre*. In Aldous Huxley's *Brave New World*, sexual freedom is obligatory; a female character is rebuked for confining her sexual relations to one man. In no time at all, family theater audiences were to be pleased and amused by an actress in the stage musical *Oklahoma* who sang *I'm Just a Girl Who Can't Say No*. Not long afterward, Vladimir Nabokov's novel *Lolita*, about a man's sexual obsession with a young girl, Philip Roth's *Portnoy's Complaint*, hilariously portraying a man's sexual difficulties, and a host of other books demonstrated that sex – magical, tragic or funny – was one of the hottest commodities serious book publishers had to peddle.

Two world wars and a handful of other conflagrations had accelerated the pace of social change, promoting the spread and intensification of sexual permissiveness. Interest in birth control (the term had been coined by feminist Margaret Sanger in 1913) spread. Contraceptives and contraceptive counseling became more readily available and utilized.

If women could fill factory and office jobs left vacant by men who went off to battle, could drive ambulances and be assigned to non-combatant military roles, even in some places be trained for combat, whatever illusions Victorians had nurtured about the purity and demureness of the female were resoundingly proved preposterous.

Young men, laboring in the shadow of earlier standards, may have been taught to croon *I Want a Girl Just Like the Girl Who Married Dear Old Dad* (oblivious of the not-so-antiseptic interpretations of this sentiment which psychologists were dredging out of the corners of psyches). What they really believed was *There is Nothing Like a Dame.*

Patriotic moralists raised no objections to the teasing pinup photos which soldiers away from home eyed with thoughts something less than chaste. Groups of traveling entertainers, officially dispatched to entertain the troops, invariably included buxom beauties for the men to ogle. When, in the Second World War, German troops sang sentimentally about *Lili Marlene*, a prostitute who stood seductively "underneath the lamp post by the barrack gate," it took on romantic proportions and crossed the lines, to be sung by men on both sides.

A degree of license had always been permitted soldiers in wartime. But never before had their experiences while in uniform had such influence on enduring popular standards. *How're You Gonna Keep Them Down on the Farm After They've Seen Paree?* asked a First World War song. The question was valid. The effect of mass communications, as well as the mass movement of armies, meant, in effect, that a great many people had "seen Paree" – either actually or metaphorically – and were, as a consequence, less prim, less straitlaced.

To a great extent, Paris had escaped the more severe ravages of Victorian prudery. That was where, early in the twentieth century, individual brothels had developed reputations for the particular unconventional sexual services in which they specialized, and where some brothels were such lucrative enterprises that they were bought and sold for huge sums of money. That was where young Leon Blum, later to be prime minister, could publicly urge men and women not to marry until they had acquired sufficient sexual experience ; where a doctor could promote the establishment of a human stud farm for young people to guarantee that their sexual fluids (damaging to health and temperament if withheld) were properly disposed of. Paris was where that restless American, Henry Miller, could compile both his extravagent sexual adventures and the books in which he described them so graphically. It was where the uproarious stage farces of Feydeau were based on the joys and delicious dangers of adultery and where the chorines of the "Folies Bergère" could, beginning in 1911, delight audiences by appearing alluringly naked on stage.

The daring displays of the beautiful "Folies" girls and coy exhibitions of striptease *artistes* were, however, to seem erotically tame as the decades passed. Bare-breasted and later "bottomless" entertainers and waitresses began to appear in restaurants and nightclubs in San Francisco, Las Vegas, Amsterdam, Copenhagen, Berlin and other cities. Toplessness and even full nudity (as an erotic fashion rather than the traditional health fetish) became a feature of certain beaches, first along the French Riviera, notably at St. Tropez.

Nudity also made much publicized appearances in the legitimate theater, in *Hair*, a celebration of the "youth culture" of the 1960s, in *Oh, Calcutta*, a sexually titillating review a few years later, and subsequently in dozens of other theatrical presentations and ballets, in some of which nudity was only very incidental to primary themes. Gradually, finding excuses for its use as a stage device became unnecessary.

During the 1960s in Copenhagen (which developed a reputation as the "sin city" of Europe), people flocked to small theaters and clubs to see young men and women copulating and mouthing each other on stage – that being the full extent of the entertainment. Private men's clubs in other places, where such public shows were illegal, legally arranged for similar private performances before audiences made up of members and invited guests.

Such clubs also provided a market for sex exploitation

movies. These "skin flicks" were usually brief, amateurishly produced films featuring a variety of sexual acts. But eroticism in the movies had a much wider and significant application and influence.

Until the invention of moving pictures in the late nineteenth century, the dissemination of erotica had basic limitations. Literary erotica was restricted not only to those who read books and articles, but also to those who were determined enough to seek out sexually provocative writings which were not always easily obtainable. Erotic painting and sculpture had an even more restricted audience. Movies were easily accessible to far more people than had ever before been exposed to erotic themes. And moving images of erotic scenes were for most people much more real and provocative. They were much more capable of stimulating the imagination of those who were timid and inhibited, as well as of everybody else.

Generally, movie pioneers did not tread too quickly into the arena of erotica. Not till the 1920s did such extravaganzas as *Belshazzar's Feast, Ben-Hur* and other epics set in the ancient world come replete with nearly naked females scattered around the screen in anticipation of orgies (which, when shown, were not at all explicit).

The movie industry soon came to be based on the star system and the stars invariably had sex appeal – Clara Bow, the original movie "vamp"; John Barrymore with his Adonis-like profile; Rudolf Valentino with his hint of erotic savagery. Movie directors gradually mastered the devices which their skills put at their disposal. At a time when prevailing standards restricted male-female contact on the commercial screen to shy kisses, John Barrymore and Theda Bara were permitted to indulge in a seemingly endless clinch which excited passions clear across America (and which was the product of four takes on camera skillfully pieced together by the movie editor).

The erotic potential of the movie industry was recognized early by influential puritanical elements which were able to impose sets of rules the industry was obliged to observe. These included the requirement that females be sufficiently attired not to appear "obscene," that twin beds be used even when husband and wife went to sleep on the screen, and that an actor keep at least one foot on the floor when involved in a bedroom scene (innocent, of course) with an actress. But erotic content was not that easily eliminated. The mere display of beautiful women and virile men stirred the emotions of millions of movie-goers.

A wide variety of moods were offered, from the playful seductiveness of Mae West ("I used to be Snow White but I drifted") to the sensual feline quality of Brigitte Bardot; from the swarthy "hunk of man" virility of Clark Gable to the suave handsomeness of Cary Grant. The stories were more often than not romantic slush, but the images on the screen were exciting in more than romantic ways.

There had, virtually from the beginning, been a small corner of the movie industry which produced undisguised erotic movies. Among the pioneers of the great German film industry early in the twentieth century were those who made such movies as *The Whore's Paradise* and *The Seduced*, pictures in which erotic content was the main focus. In the 1930s, pioneering French movie-makers also produced movies with distinctly uncamouflaged sexual scenes.

Erotically stimulating "stag" pictures, produced for distribution to private clubs and individuals, were made in many countries. But not until after the Second World War did the explicitly erotic element make a forceful appearance in widely released feature movies, reaching a point where the Italian director Pasolini could trace provocative themes with great flair and aesthetic imagination in his cinematographic interpretation of Boccaccio's *Decameron*. Still more imaginative was the brilliant *Last Tango in Paris*, a very successful movie commercially which, despite its reputation for lewdness, may have been the first representation of the sexual act as an expression of deeply moving grief.

But, generally, erotic displays on the movie screen were not keyed to that superior level. They were usually, at best, only sensually provocative, often mindlessly so, despite occasional

185

gestures at giving them social or intellectual significance. But more and more movie-goers seemed to be satisfied with such fare and as purely pornographic pictures became increasingly lucrative propositions, a growing number of movie-houses sought to recapture lost audiences – largely won over by television – by showing *Confessions of a Nymphomaniac, Redlight Girls* and other such erotic romps.

Erotica reached television vicariously. The late-night showing of old movies with mildly erotic content was the way it started though occasional television plays began to inch in the 1970s along the same ground the movies had worked across two decades earlier. They played around the edges of specific sexuality, flashing a bosom here and a passionate kiss there and even, with discreet camera work, a hint of the act of copulation. Barring a resurgence of puritanism, it is likely that in the not-too-distant future, television will overcome existing restraints, at least during the late hours of the night, when children are presumed to be safely and innocently abed.

Far more than any previous period, the twentieth century has been an age of analysis and introspection. Modern men and women have devoted vast amounts of thought, time and energy to exploring human behavior, interpreting characteristics and motives, compiling surveys, asking intimate questions, drawing conclusions – taking the erotic measure of mankind.

Some of this analysis has been shallow generality of the "Latins are Lousy Lovers" and "Most Women Don't Have Orgasms!" variety. But there has also been an impressive number of meaningful, meticulous studies, including those produced by scientifically oriented institutes for the study of sexuality which have sprung up in various places in the world as if to indicate that this is an idea whose time has come.

This century had barely begun when an inkling of what was to come might have been derived from the recognition accorded to theories of sexuality formulated by English psychologist and physician Havelock Ellis. In seven remarkable volumes, *Studies of the Psychology of Sex*, Ellis paved the way toward making examination of the erotic terrain respectable for scientists and scholars. His explorations dealt with such once murky regions as sexual impulse, distinctive characteristics of sexual desire and performance in men and women, the "erogenic" zones, homosexuality and sexual morality.

Among the many daring conclusions drawn by Ellis: male impotence and female frigidity are usually of psychological origin; "the distribution of the sexual impulse between the two sexes is fairly balanced"; multiple orgasms are common with women; the female's sexual impulse is more likely to need external arousal and the female orgasm develops more slowly than that of the male; men and women can remain sexually active past middle age. But a major thrust of Ellis's presentation was that there is no such thing as "normal" sexual behavior: people are different and their sexual responses and performances are different. (Ellis's personal stake in establishing that sexual normality is a myth was revealed in an autobiography in which he disclosed that he himself had been unable to enjoy sexual fulfillment until he was sixty years old and that he had suffered for some three decades from "copious nocturnal emissions.")

Of even greater and more resounding impact were the theories of Sigmund Freud. Defying the outrage, contempt and mockery of his colleagues in the medical profession in his native Vienna and elsewhere in central Europe, Freud wove together a series of explanations for the origin and character of sexual drives which, he decreed, were crucial ingredients in the way human behavior is fashioned. Those drives, he said, begin with babies already endowed with in-built erotic impulses which develop along generally decipherable patterns as the infant became a child, the child became an adolescent, and the adolescent became an adult. Freud contended that infantile sexual desires usually were repressed (the civilizing process) but later manifested themselves in different forms.

Sexual drives were, according to Freud, at first oral, characterized by a baby's biting and sucking. Then their primary focus was anal and, ultimately, in the course of development,

they centered on the genital regions. Freud also was responsible for wide circulation of the theory of some of his teachers
and predecessors that the particular erotic inclinations of an
individual could reflect traumatic early experiences which
interrupted normal development and left enduring psychic
marks.

Freud's analyses traced a wide range of behavior patterns
back to sexual experience or sexual drive. These included
penis-envy of women (among the theories for which he would
later be condemned and derided by feminists and others) and
Oedipal conflicts between fathers and sons.

Freud's theories were dismissed as fantasies by most of his
colleagues. One of them suggested, in all seriousness, that
they were more suitably a matter for police investigation than
for medical study. But those theories opened the gates to a
deluge of psychological probings of the sexual content of
human aspirations and actions.

Freud was succeeded by other explorers of the human
psyche, with other interpretations of sexual impulses. Many
were former advocates of Freudian dogmas, men and women
who produced their own explanations for the origins of
human erotic responses. These included Wilhelm Reich who
insisted there was an indelible link between the social and
sexual shortcomings of civilization and that revolutions in
both spheres were essential before men and women could be
truly liberated. (Reich also developed theories concerning the
proper expenditure of sexual energy and discovered the
"orgone" life force. This, he insisted, was present everywhere
and could be accumulated by individuals who spent time in a
large metal box called an "orgone energy accumulator" – the
promotion of which led to the tragic farce of Reich's imprisonment in the United States for selling fraudulent medical
equipment. He died in prison.)

Others went in different directions in search of sexual
understanding. Cultural anthropologists like Bronislaw
Malinowski and Margaret Mead studied the ways of peoples
of Pacific islands and other places who have managed to avoid
the full benefits of the modern world and they emerged with

intriguing analyses of sexual practices of primitive societies. And those who probed the human psyche and primitive communities for new insights into sexual behavior were, in turn, succeeded by a different category of sex researcher, people like Alfred Kinsey, and Masters and Johnson, who sought, in effect, to take the sexual pulse of cross-sections of people to describe what was actually transpiring, rather than to unearth motives and origins.

Although others had tentatively explored the path he followed, Kinsey's *Sexual Behavior of the Human Male*, which appeared in 1948, and his *Sexual Behavior of the Human Female*, which appeared five years later, were pioneer works. They established a statistical approach to erotic behavior. They initiated a new form of sexual sociology, replete with charts, tables and percentages. One commentator said, "The Kinsey Report did for sex what Columbus did for geography."

The two Kinsey studies collated the behavioral patterns of more than 12,000 women and men of various ages, geographical regions, religions and marital statuses. Among the conclusions: 92 percent of men and 62 percent of women masturbated at some point in their lives; 86 percent of men under thirty and almost half the women interviewed had engaged in premarital intercourse. About 40 percent of married men had been sexually unfaithful to their wives; 37 percent of men and 28 percent of women admitted to having had homosexual relations at one time or another. One out of every six farmboys had "experienced orgasm as the product of animal contacts."

Despite some telling criticism of Kinsey's interview methods (his was neither a random sample nor a carefully chosen cross-section – a high proportion of those he interviewed were volunteers and presumably had more strongly held views on sex than most people), his conclusions had an extraordinary effect. If they indicated that as many as nine out of every ten men engaged in some form of what was, strictly speaking, illegal sexual activity, and if substantial numbers of men and women did things which prevailing public standards dubbed obscene or wrong, those standards clearly were out of touch.

William Masters and Virginia Johnson, in their *Human Sexual Response* (published in 1966) took matters a step further. Through careful observation under laboratory conditions of thousands of male and female orgasms, they offered evidence that the orgasm was a physiological event to which just about everybody had joyful access (that, for example, sexual frigidity can be overcome and that penis size can be irrelevant to sexual pleasure). The debate was shifting from whether sex was right or wrong to proper ways of achieving the sexual satisfaction everyone deserves.

The second half of the twentieth century has thus seen the launching of sexologists as respected scientific researchers. Some of them who ventured into the sphere of popular science, and made their conclusions coherent to the man in the street, earned the kind of recognition (and reward) few scientific investigators can normally hope to receive. There was no stopping the flood of literature devoted to sex as a statistical, medical and social phenomenon. The type of orgasm, the frequency of masturbation, the preferred positions for copulation – collated by social class and education level – all these and more became subjects of serious study and analysis.

The extension and depth of popular sexual interest stimulated a need and desire for greater sex education than had previously been available. From cautious, grudging tolerance early in the twentieth century for lectures on "responsibilities" in marriage, there developed – very gradually at first, and then helter-skelter – a much more direct approach to teaching people what sex is all about.

It remains, however, a delicate subject, not easily broached, particularly with school children. A "birds-and-bees" approach to where babies came from was only slowly replaced with a more specific, but still cautiously antiseptic physiological analysis. The structure of the genitals was examined. The physiological significance and consequences were explained in school. But residual restraints were very much in evidence. There was, for example, rarely any consideration of the pleasure and other emotional aspects of sexual indulgence. This shortcoming was partly remedied in some frank, often well-illustrated children's books, like *Where Did I Come From?* by Peter Mayle (1973), which explains:

> The man loves the woman. So he gives her a kiss. And she gives him a kiss. And they hug each other very tight. And after a while, the man's penis becomes stiff and hard and much bigger than it usually is. It gets bigger because it has lots of work to do. . . . The man wants to get as close to the woman as he can, because he's feeling very loving to her. And to get really close the best thing he can do is lie on top of her and put his penis inside her, into her vagina. Making love . . . is a very nice feeling for both the man and the woman. He likes being inside her, and she likes him being inside her.

The charm of such a recital is rarely to be found in adult sex manuals which make little mention of affection except, occasionally, in the most mechanical fashion. To some observers, this seemed to reflect a growing force-of-habit attitude to sex generally, masking a persistent underlying bewilderment.

In *The Folklore of Sex* in 1951, Albert Ellis said most of us are "completely muddled-, mixed-, and messed-up" in our sex views, feelings and acts. Writing about America (in a description presumably applicable to other places as well) in *The Feminine Mystique* some two decades later, Betty Friedan complained, "Sex . . . is becoming a strangely joyless national compulsion . . . The sex-glutted novels become increasingly explicit and increasingly dull . . . The endless flow of manuals describing new sex techniques hint at an endless lack of excitement."

Such gloomy assessments were not without a fair measure of truth. But they were not meant to be, nor did they add up to, a convincing denunciation of the broadened climate of erotic opportunity – any more than gluttony and oafishness at the dinner table can be attributed to an abundance of food. The heart of the matter is that we have not yet resolved the sex conundrum. There's really no telling whether we ever will.

From *Patterns of Sexual Behavior*,
by Clellan S. Ford and Frank A. Beach (1951)

. . . heterosexual coitus is the prevalent form of sexual activity for adults of all human societies and of all mammalian species. All mammals except man customarily copulate in a rear entry position; exceptions are rare. By contrast, there is no known human society in which rear entry is the usual pattern of intercourse. The universality of some variant of face-to-face intercourse in human beings reflects in part the anatomical fact that the vaginal opening of the human female is farther forward than it is in other mammals. Face-to-face copulation affords a better opportunity for intense stimulation of the woman's sexual organs, particularly the clitoris, than does rear entry, and is therefore more apt to bring her to orgasm. In this connection it is of importance to note that positive indication of a sexual climax has not been detected in females of any infra-human species. This emphasizes the possibility that stimulation of the clitoris plays a highly significant role in female sexuality, since intercourse with rear entry gives no opportunity for direct clitoral stimulation.

From *Lady Chatterley's Lover* **(1928), by D.H. Lawrence**

He took her in his arms again and drew her to him, and suddenly she became small in his arms, small and nestling. It was gone, the resistance was gone, and she began to melt in a marvellous peace. And as she melted small and wonderful in his arms, she became infinitely desirable to him, all his blood vessels seemed to scald with intense yet tender desire, for her, for her softness, for the penetrating beauty of her in his arms, passing in his blood. And softly, with that marvellous swoon-like caress of his hand in pure soft desire, softly he stroked the silky slope of her loins, down, down between her soft warm buttocks, coming nearer and nearer to the very quick of her. And she felt him like a flame of desire, yet tender, and she felt herself melting in the flame. She let herself go. She felt his penis risen against her with silent amazing force and asser-tion, and she let herself go to him. She yielded with a quiver that was like death, she went all open to him. And oh, if he were not tender to her now, how cruel, for she was all open to him and helpless! She quivered again at the potent inexorable entry inside her, so strange and terrible. It might come with the thrust of a sword in her softly-opened body, and that would be death. She clung in a sudden anguish of terror. But it came with a strange slow thrust of peace, the dark thrust of peace and a ponderous, primordial tenderness . . .

From *Studies in the Psychology of Sex* **(1913), by Havelock Ellis**

We see that there are . . . two constituents in (sexual) impulse . . . They are . . . so intimately connected as to form two distinct stages in the same process: a first stage, in which – usually under the parallel influence of internal and external stimuli – images, desires and ideals grow up within the mind, while the organism generally is charged with energy and the sexual apparatus congested with blood; and a second stage, in which the sexual apparatus is discharged amid profound sexual excitement, followed by deep organic relief. By the first process is constituted the tension which the second process relieves . . . The first, taking on usually a more active form in the male, has the double object of bringing the male himself into the condition in which discharge becomes imperative, and at the same time arousing in a female a similar ardent state of emotional excitement and sexual turgescence. The second process has the object, directly, of discharging the tension thus produced and, indirectly, of effecting the act by which the race is propagated. It seems to me that this is at present the most satisfactory way in which we can attempt to define the sexual impulse.

From *Studs Lonigan* **(1932), by James T. Farrell**

He kissed her. Her lips were feverish, and they excited him so that he roughly clutched her, clenched her firmly, and their bodies strained in an awkward embrace. Unable to check himself, he pushed her down on the couch, and pressed against her . . . She became like an instrument in his hands, quivering to his touch, panting from his heedlessly indelicate pressures and nervous hands.

"You're getting your dress all mussed," he said in uneven breaths.

"That's because of you, but I love you," she said, clenching her arms around him and straining herself until she lay on her back with him above her. Her body was strong, hard . . . She scratched his neck, pulling his face down to kiss him. She bit his lip . . . He fumbled, trying to remove her dress.

"Just a minute," she gasped.

Studs sat beside her, humiliatingly impassioned, his hands almost trembling, and he felt that he must look like a fool to her. She sat up, smiling painfully . . .

She arose and he felt it was goodbye. She pulled her dress over her head. He leaped to her and pulled it off. He quickly removed his coat, tie, shoes, socks and shorts, and looked at her partially nude in the semi-darkness. He choked with pride. She was doing this because of him, passion for him, because of his kisses, his touches, himself. She lay down wantonly, and like a grateful puppy he kissed her gently. She held him against her, and he could feel the warmth of her flesh. He tore wildly at the straps of her undergarment.

From *The Encyclopedia of Psychology* **(1946)**
Editors: H.J. Eysenck, W. Arnold, R. Meili

Orgasm, physiology of. Orgasm is the climax of sexual excitement and reaction which can be induced by any effective form of somatosexual or psychosexual stimulation. It represents an abrupt, involuntary discharge of psychophysical and neuromuscular tensions and is probably accompanied by reactions in all organs and organ systems of the body. Findings to date suggest that in any physiological definition of the orgasm in man or woman the following reactions need to be stressed: (a) peak intensity of sexual pleasure; (b) involuntary muscular contractions in the genital and anal areas and many extra-genital muscle groups; (c) concentration of blood both in the genital area (e.g. vagina or penis) and outside them; (d) culmination of the reactions of heart, circulation and respiration; (e) partial or total loss of sensory capacities and at times loss of consciousness for a matter of seconds or minutes. Characteristic of orgasm are the contractions of the orgasmic platform in woman and of ejaculation in man. In physical responses (apart from ejaculation), orgasm in woman resembles that in man. The following specific differences have, however, been described. A woman's subjective feelings during orgasm are more variable than a man's. The orgasm usually lasts longer in woman who, unlike man, can achieve additional orgasms immediately after the first. Moreover, more women than men need to experience a number of orgasms before achieving satisfaction. In general, women appear to possess greater capacity, both quantitative and qualitative, for orgiastic response.

From *Ulysses* (1921), by James Joyce

By what reflections did he, a conscious reactor against the void of uncertitude, justify to himself his sentiments?

The preordained frangibility of the hymen, the pre-supposed intangibility of the thing in itself: the incongruity and disproportion between the selfprolonging tension of the thing proposed to be done and the selfabbreviating relaxation of the thing done: the fallaciously inferred debility of the female, the muscularity of the male: the variations of ethical codes. . . .

The visible signs of antesatisfaction?

An approximate erection: a solicitous adversion: a gradual elevation: a tentative revelation: a silent contemplation.

Then?

He kissed the plump mellow yellow smellow melons of her rump, on each plump melonous hemisphere, in their mellow yellow furrow, with obscure prolonged provacative melon-smellonous osculation.

The visible signs of postsatisfaction?

A silent contemplation: a tentative velation: a gradual abasement: a solicitous aversion: a proximate erection.

In Prospect

. . . between now and the twenty-first century, millions of ordinary, psychologically normal people will face an abrupt collision with the future.

— ALVIN TOFFLER, *Future Shock*

IN JULY 1978, the birth of a baby girl in Oldham, England, opened a new chapter in history. Because of irregularities in the mother's Fallopian tubes, doctors had removed sperm from the father and used it to fertilize an extracted ovum from the mother in a laboratory dish. They then reinserted the fertilized ovum into the mother's womb where it successfully continued its embryonic growth and development until it emerged – normal, healthy and howling – into the light of the world in a routine hospital delivery. The first "test-tube baby" had been born.

It was a momentous event in the annals of sexuality. It meant that after millions of years, humans could be conceived and born, and the survival of the human race could be guaranteed, without the insertion of a single penis into a single vagina. What is more, genetic engineers are working on ways to expand test-tube baby techniques to eliminate in the "test-tube" stage various genetic disabilities which can afflict babies. There is still a long way to go before the process is perfected. Some setbacks are inevitable. But it could prove to be a more efficient (and more reliable) means of perpetuating a healthy human race than copulation ever was. As a baby-

198

making device, sex could, with the passage of time, become passé.

Normally when things lose their function or are improved upon, they cease to exist, gradually wither away or, like the human appendix, they languish. If it were something other than it is, sex – shorn of its practical, biological purpose – might also be on its way to becoming obsolete. However, it remains uniquely pleasurable, with or without the procreative function, and patently not about to fade away. Though designed by nature as an incentive for procreation, sexual pleasure long ago became a distinct function in itself – albeit confined and badgered by restrictive functional social codes.

But disruptive problems of the community today result primarily from economic and social quandaries which have little to do with erotic inclinations. And staggering divorce rates (one divorce for every two marriages in the United States in 1977; in the Soviet Union, one out of every three couples married that year were divorced) testify that the family is already in deep trouble, largely for non-sexual reasons.

A key factor in the fragility of marriage is the unreliable romantic ingredient which some time ago became central to the commonly accepted western image of the proper husband-wife relationship. Romantic love more often than not is short-lived. When it fizzles out, marriages rooted in such love are fundamentally undermined and have little reason to continue. This process has been promoted of late by the emergence of batteries of helpful specialists – psychologists, social workers, government welfare payment officials – to play many of the key traditional counseling, supportive and protective functions of the spouse.

No doubt the changing sexual climate has also played an important role. One sociologist reflected recognition and acceptance of greater sexual opportunities by describing marriage as "a form of sexual malnutrition." But other factors predominate in the breakdown of the marriage institution.

It is increasingly evident that the original family-protecting, community-welfare purposes for restricting sexual freedom are losing their relevance. As the intensifying sexual climate indicates, it is they, rather than sex, which are becoming obsolete. Their obsolescence is the chief catalyst of the modern sexual revolution which is shaping up as vestiges of the sex-is-bad, sex-might-be-bad morality expire.

There could, of course, be a backlash. Many advocates of measures to restrain and police the erotic environment have warned that the alternative is irreparable disruption of the harmony and well-being of the community as a whole. They say a permissive sexual revolution is not inevitable; that their crusade is not futile; that permissive periods have flourished and then subsided in the past; that a time for renewed sexual restraints will soon again be upon us.

But there are basic unprecedented developments ushering in the sexual revolution and these are unlikely to be soon swamped by a new wave of moralistic fervor. Contraception is effective. Venereal disease can be controlled. Social disapproval of sexual adventure by females is on the decline amidst indications that such a development is much more than temporary fashion. Moreover, residual feelings of sexual guilt or extreme modesty are increasingly considered neurotic and remediable. Casual sexual indulgence and temporary marriages of various durations (both formal and common law) are increasingly common. A recent survey indicated that 13 percent of all Danish couples live together without having been formally married and, presumably, could separate as unceremoniously.

A new, revolutionary sexual climate is distinctly in the making. It could, of course, channel sex into less traditional directions. Almost as if anticipating an imminent termination of the crucial link between heterosexual sex and the perpetuation of the species, homosexuality has become a much more dynamic and conspicuous movement over the last two decades. In parts of the United States, male "gays" have been organized into the first sexually oriented political force in history.

At the same time, some radical feminists have been suggesting that men could (and should) become superfluous to the sex needs of women. Some have insisted that the penis does not usually stimulate orgasms in women because, anatomically, it is not up to the job. In the words of one feminist, ". . . lesbian sexuality, in rubbing one clitoris against the other, could make an excellent case, based on anatomical data, for the extinction of male organs."

But the overwhelming majority of men and women remain heterosexual and show little sign of wanting to change. They both will, however, have to come to terms with the enormous sexual implications of the women's liberation movement. A goodly number of females – particularly younger ones – are already determined not to be, or appear to be, subservient to men, or subject to the sexual whims of men, or compelled to keep their own sexual impulses in demure harness until aroused by men. The sexually assertive female, a comic figure until now, will be part of the brave, new, hopefully unneurotic world looming on the horizon.

There will be problems of adjustment. As Ira Reiss pointed out in *The Encyclopedia of Sexual Behavior*, "We are in a state of transition and those who cling to the past get hurt by the customs of the present and those who rush to the future are damaged by the traditions of the past." But that has always been true in the course of cultural development.

Even before we have successfully come to terms with the changes now taking place, we may have an even greater erotic adjustment to make. Scientists have been toying with a wide range of drugs which can control human feelings and emotional responses. They have been exploring the brain with remarkable thoroughness. One day in the not-too-distant future, they will fathom exactly which electrical charges and chemical changes in our brain cells produce sexual ecstasy, and how it happens. Not along after, they will concoct a drug for generating sexual pleasure – a pill or potion with directions on the bottle listing dosages required for producing the various degrees and kinds of erotic satisfaction.

After all that men and women have been through in the development of sexuality over the ages, the great irony would be for the medical substitute to prove more exciting, more pleasurable, and more exalting than the real thing.

Selected Reading

A selected list of sources consulted in preparation of this book:

Acton, Wm., *The Functions and Disorders of the Reproductive Organs*

Apuleius, Lucius, *The Golden Ass*

Aristaenetus, *The Love Epistles*

Aristophanes, *Complete Plays*

Ardrey, Robert, *The Hunting Hypothesis*

Balsdon, J.P., *Roman Women*

Bassermann, Lujo, *The Oldest Profession*

Bloch, Ivan, *Sexual Life in England*

Boehn, M. von, *Modes and Manners*

Brander, M., *The Victorian Gentleman*

Brantome, *Lives of Fair and Gallant Ladies*

Briffault, Robert, *The Mothers*

Bullough, Vern and Bonnie, *Sin, Sickness and Sanity*

Burford, E.J., *The 'Orrible Synne*

Calhoun, A.W., *A Social History of the American Family*

Casanova, Giacomo, *Memoirs*

Chaucer, Geoffrey, *Canterbury Tales*

Clark, Kenneth, *The Nude*

Cleland, John, *Fanny Hill*

Cleugh, James, *Love Locked Out*

Cohn, Norman, *The Pursuit of the Millenium*

Comfort, Alex, *The Anxiety Makers*

Comfort, Alex, *The Joy of Sex*

Darlington, C.D., *The Evolution of Man and Society*

Dingwall, Eric J., *The American Woman*

Dingwall, Eric J., *The Girdle of Chastity*

Ditzion, Sidney, *Marriage, Morals and Sex in America*

Dover, K.J., *Classical Greek Attitudes to Sexual Behavior*

Eibl-Eibesfeldt, Irenaeus, *Love and Hate*

Ellis, Albert, *The Folklore of Sex*

Ellis, Havelock, *Studies in the Psychology of Sex*

Erlanger, Philip, *The Age of Courts and Kings*

Erman, Adolf, *The Ancient Egyptians*

Forberg, F.K., *Manual of Classical Erotology*

Ford, Clellan and Beach, Frank, *Patterns of Sexual Behavior*

Frazer, Sir James, *The Golden Bough*

Freud, Sigmund, *Basic Writings*

Friedan, Betty, *The Feminine Mystique*

Fryer, Peter, *Mrs. Grundy — Studies in English Prudery*

Goncourt, Edmund and Jules de, *Women of the 18th Century*

Green, V.H.H., *Medieval*

Civilization in Western Europe

Harrison, Fraser, *The Dark Angel: Aspects of Victorian Sexuality*

Himes, N.E., *Medical History of Contraception*

Huizinga, Johan, *The Waning of the Middle Ages*

Hunt, Morton, *The Natural History of Love*

Hyde, H. Montgomery, *A History of Pornography*

James, E.O., *Cult of the Mother Goddess*

James, E.O., *Marriage and Society*

Juvenal, *Satires*

Kaster, J., *Literature and Mythology of Ancient Egypt*

Kinsey, Alfred, *Sexual Behavior in the Human Female*

Kinsey, Alfred, *Sexual Behavior in the Human Male*

Krafft-Ebing, Richard, *Psychopathia Sexualis*

Kramer, S.N., *History Begins at Sumer*

Lambert, W.G., *Morals in Ancient Mesopotamia* in *Ex Orient Lux* (1957–8)

Laver, James, *The Age of Illusion*

Lea, H.C., *Sacerdotal Celibacy*

Lecky, W.E.H., *History of European Morals*

Leroi-Gourhan, André, *The Art of Prehistoric Man in Western Europe*

Lewinsohn, Richard, *A History of Sexual Customs*

Licht, Hans, *Sexual Life in Ancient Greece*

Lindsay, Jack, *The Ancient World*

Lucian, *The Dialogues*

MacCary, James, *Human Sexuality*

Machiavelli, Niccolo, *Mandrake*

Mantegazza, Paolo, *The Sexual Relations of Mankind*

Marcus, Steven, *The Other Victorians*

Masters, Wm. H. and Johnson, Virginia E., *Human Sexual Inadequacy*

Masters, Wm. H. and Johnson, Virginia, E., *Human Sexual Response*

May, Geoffrey, *Social Control of Sex Expression*

McQueen, James, *Babylon*

Millet, Kate, *Sexual Politics*

Morris, Desmond, *The Naked Ape*

O'Neill, W.L., *The American Sexual Dilemma*

Ovid, *The Art of Love*

Pearsall, Ronald, *Worm in the Bud*

Pearson, L., *Popular Ethics in Ancient Greece*

Pepys, Samuel, *Diaries*

Pike, E. Royston, *Love in Ancient Rome*

Plato, *The Symposium*

Pomeroy, Sarah, *Goddesses, Whores, Wives and Slaves*

Propertius, *The Elegies*

Richardson, Joanna, *The Courtesans*

Riencourt, Amaury de, *Sex and Power in History*

Rose, Alfred, *Registrum Librorum Eroticum*

Rochester, Earl of, *Poems*

Saggs, H.W.F., *The Greatness That Was Babylon*

Seward, Desmond, *Prince of the Renaissance*

Stone, Lawrence, *The Family, Sex*

and Marriage in England
1500–1800

Suetonius, *The Lives of the Twelve
Caesars*

Taylor, G. Rattray, *Sex in History*

Toffler, Alvin, *Future Shock*

Trudgill, Eric, *Madonnas and
Magdalenas*

Turner, E.S., *A History of
Courting*

Twain, Mark, *1601*

Valency, Maurice, *In Praise of
Love*

Van de Velde, Th. H., *Ideal
Marriage*

Walters, Margaret, *The Nude
Male*

Washburn, S.L., *Social Life of
Early Man*

Webb, Peter, *The Erotic Arts*

Westermarck, Edward, *History of
Human Marriage*

Wilkes, John, *An Essay on Woman*

Young, Wayland, *Eros Denied*

Zeldin, Theodore, *Ambition, Love
and Politics*

Picture Credits

Page 14: Female figure from Hagar Qim in Malta. Late third millenium BC. Displays vestiges of earlier exaggerated characteristics of feminine imagery which became less common as civilization planted roots. Archaeological Museum, Valetta, Malta.

Page 15: The Venus of Vestonice, from the late Stone Age. Like other prehistoric "Venuses" unearthed by archaeologists, she reveals an aspect of the sexual imagination of prehistoric humans. Moravian Museum, Brno, Czechoslovakia.

Page 26: Giant of Cerne Abbas, Dorset, England. Figure cut into hillside. Second century A.D. Even in recent times, local women who had been unable to become pregnant through other means sometimes camped overnight on its phallus. Aerofilms.

Page 27: Egyptian girl holding a lute, from a tomb painting in Thebes. Sexually stimulating art offended no conventions in ancient Egypt, where erotica was frequently blended into religious legend.

Page 40: Satyr from ancient Greece. One of the group of lecherous minor deities who accompanied Dionysus, god of wine and revelry. Origin of the word *satyriasis*: abnormal sexual desire by a man for women. National Museum, Athens.

Page 41: Orgy scene on Greek vase. The orgy was an accepted Greek diversion even in respectable circles. Great skill was employed in the service of the erotic arts in ancient Greece. Louvre Museum, Paris.

Page 62: Roman floor mosaic. Many of the villas of wealthier Romans were decorated with such usually playful scenes. Photo-resources.

Page 63: Bacchanalian dance, from a wall painting in a Roman villa. Such libidinous scenes were enacted at annual festivals which were often characterized by orgiastic displays. Werner Forman Archive.

Page 86: Woman wearing chastity belt. Husband at left, lover, with key, at right. Chastity belts were sometimes artistically engraved and cushioned with fine fabric.

Page 87: Man and woman together in a bathtub. A medieval German scene. There was restraint and often great simplicity to medieval erotica.

Page 104: *Allegory of Passion* by Bronzino. In addition to the exquisite artistry of Renaissance erotica, it bubbled with the sense of liberation that characterized the times. National Gallery, London.

Page 105: *Venus and Mars* by Sandro Botticelli, Sculptural boldness, physical beauty and not-so-subtle sensual suggestion marked many Renaissance masterpieces. National Gallery, London.

Page 124: *Venus and Vulcan* by François Boucher. The artist displays a tender fondness for, and appreciation of, the naked female form. Wallace Collection, London.

Page 125: *Sleeping Nymph Surprised by Satyr* after Nicolas Poussin. A blend of delicacy and sensuality that marked the frequent excursions of master artists into the realm of erotica. National Gallery, London.

Page 146: Illustration for *Lysistrata* by Aubrey Beardsley. An almost mocking dimension of erotica, accentuated by excellent drafts-manship.

Page 147: Victorian book illustration. Artist unknown. Uncharacteristic sentimentality in an age when erotica tended usually to be less delicate. Sara Lee private collection.

Page 172: From *Unter Vier Augen* (1908) by Reznicek. Modern sophistication enlisted in the service of sexual arousal. Mary Evans Picture Library.

Page 173: *The Lovely Wave*. Turn of the century magazine illustration. A forerunner of the modern pinup. Mansell Collection.

Index

208